FIFTH EDITION

Understanding

INDUSTRY

now

GW00402309

FIFTH EDITION

Understanding

INDUSTRY

now

ROSEMARIE STEFANOU

foreword by Sir John Harvey-Jones

UI

Hodder & Stoughton

A MEMBER OF THE HODDER HEADLINE GROUP

Authors Acknowledgements

My special thanks go to my husband, Stelio Stefanou of John Doyle Group PLC, without whose help and advice I could not have written this book. I would also like to thank those who provided me with much useful information in this fifth edition: Elissa Armstrong and Sally Stokes of 3i; Jan Buckingham of Allied Lyons; Stuart Pearcey of British Steel at Scunthorpe; John Bevan and Margaret Hedges of Sony Manufacturing Company UK; David Dimmock of Standard Life; Kathleen Duncan of TSB Foundation; Frank Woodcock of Toshiba Consumer Products; Graham Parker of United Biscuits; Ken Davies of Vauxhall Motors; Mo Foster of Virgin Management Limited.

A catalogue for this title is available from the British Library.

ISBN UI 0 340 62739 5
ISBN Hodder & Stoughton 0 340 63138 4

First published 1989
Second edition 1991
Third edition 1992
Fourth edition 1993

First published by Hodder & Stoughton Educational 1994

Impression number	10	9	8	7	6	5	4	3	2	
Year		1999	1998	1997	1996	1995				

Typeset by Wearset, Boldon, Tyne and Wear.
Printed in Great Britain for Hodder & Stoughton Educational, a division of Hodder Headline Plc, 338 Euston Road, London NW1 3BH by The Bath Press, Lower Bristol Road, Bath.

Contents

Introduction
STANDARD LIFE

Marketing and Sales

Design and Development SONY

Production
UB
United Biscuits

Personnel
TSB

Finance
Lloyds Bank

Management
ALLIED LYONS

Small Business

Logos of firms and organisations referred to in this book

The authors would like to thank the following firms and organisations for their help in supplying information and/or photographs:

3i Plc

Cadbury Limited

Glaxo Pharmaceuticals UK Limited

Lloyds Bank Plc

Sony United Kingdom Limited
SONY

3M United Kingdom Plc
3M

Chartered Institute of Marketing

Grand Metropolitan Plc
GRAND METROPOLITAN
adding value

Michael Peters Limited

Standard Life Assurance Company
STANDARD LIFE

Advertising Association

The Advertising Association

Clarks International

Hewlett-Packard Limited
 HEWLETT PACKARD

Nuclear Electric Plc
 **Nuclear Electric**
CLEAN ENERGY FOR THE 21ST CENTURY

Tesco Stores Ltd
 TESCO

Airdata Limited
**AirData**

Confederation of British Industry
CBI

IBM United Kingdom Limited
IBM

Oxford Magnet Technology Limited
OXFORD

Texas Instruments
 TEXAS INSTRUMENTS

Allied Lyons

ALLIED LYONS

Department of Employment
 **EMPLOYMENT DEPARTMENT**

Imperial Chemical Industries Plc
 ICI

Racal Electronics Group
RACAL

Toshiba Consumer Products (UK) Limited
TOSHIBA

Apple Computer UK Ltd

Department of Trade and Industry
dti

J C Bamford Excavators Limited
JCB

Renishaw Plc
 RENISHAW.

TSB Bank Plc
TSB

APV Plc
 APV

Derwent Valley Foods Limited

J Walter Thompson Company Ltd

Richer Sounds Plc
RICHER Sounds
THE UK'S BIGGEST HI-FI RETAILER - and we still put the customer first!

Unilever Plc
 U Unilever

The BOC Group Plc
 THE BOC GROUP

Design Council
THE **DESIGN** COUNCIL

Johnson Matthey
JM

Rolls Royce Plc
 ROLLS ROYCE

United Biscuits (UK) Limited
 UB
United Biscuits

The British Petroleum Company Plc
BP

Ford Motor Company Limited
 Ford

Kodak Limited
Kodak

UB (Ross Young's) Ltd
Ross Young's

Vauxhall Motors Limited
 **VAUXHALL**

The Body Shop International Plc
 THE BODY SHOP

GEC Marconi Limited
GEC-Marconi

Legal and General Group Plc
Legal & General

Rover Group Ltd
LAND ROVER | ROVER

Virgin Management Limited
Virgin

British Steel Plc
 S British Steel

GKN Plc

Levi Strauss (UK) Limited
Levi's

SmithKline Beecham
SB **SmithKline Beecham** *Nutritional Healthcare*

Volvo Car UK Limited
VOLVO

Brooke Bond Foods Limited
 *Brooke Bond Foods Ltd*

Introduction

Understanding *Industry*

Stuart Bishell

Understanding Industry Now celebrates its sixth year in publication, with over 150,000 copies distributed to students. Its comprehensive overview of how companies operate, combined with its contemporary and lively style, continue to make it a valuable asset to all students of industry and commerce.

The content has been considerably updated and the layout has been revised for the fifth edition. Once again we are grateful to all the companies who have contributed to the book, whose support enables bridges to be successfully built between education and industry.

I hope you find the book informative, involving, and indeed inspiring. The UI mission is to ensure that industry is fully understood amongst students which is critically important to our society. Understanding Industry is a key means of meeting this exciting challenge.

Stuart Bishell
Chief Executive
Understanding Industry

About UI

'Understanding Industry Now' was initiated by the Understanding Industry Trust. The Trust seeks to increase knowledge, enhance skills and improve attitudes towards industry and commerce through the delivery of unique and high quality programmes designed to inform, involve and inspire 16–19 year old students. Industry is brought into the classroom by Understanding Industry through the promotion of partnerships between business and education. The programmes are led by local business managers and emphasise student participation and practical experience. It is UI's goal that, before leaving school or college, every 16–19 year old student should have access to one of its courses.

For more information about UI and its work please contact

Understanding Industry
Enterprise House
59–65 Upper Ground
London SE1 9PQ
Tel: 071 620 0735

AEB assessment of Enhanced Course

In conjunction with the Understanding Industry Trust, the Associated Examining Board (AEB) has developed a test for sixth-form students following the Understanding Industry Enhanced Course, the syllabus of which is based on this book. The assessment consists of a one and a quarter hour test containing structured, short answer questions and is available in May annually. Schools and colleges wishing to enter candidates for the test should make their entries in the usual manner, with the AEB (tel: 0483 506506, Ext. 2342).

Foreword

Sir John Harvey-Jones

Those of us who make our lives in Industry in Britain have long seen the need to attract the brightest and best of our people to choose our way of life for a career.

Just as important is the need for those who don't join us to understand and value industry and commerce in terms of its language, ethos and method of operation.

Now, more than ever, industry is an international affair. The success of any business, no matter how small, can only be achieved in the face of intense competition from other countries. Ultimately the success of our society and our ability to create the wealth needed in order to enable us to have choices, to improve our social and health services and the standards of education in this country, depend on our being the 'best' industrially.

The problem of attracting the best to this important task is the apparently simple one of explaining what business is about and what industry, with all its myriad of challenges and opportunities, offers to, and demands of, people.

It is extraordinarily difficult for a young person to get a perspective and understanding of the richness of our life, and we industrialists have not been very good at explaining why we devote so much of ourselves so willingly and happily to this cause.

This book is aimed at helping to bridge this gap. We believe that we have nothing to lose and everything to gain from a better understanding by young people of the basis of business and the roles of such skills as marketing, production, personnel management and accounting in this continuously changing world. It is vital to get each of this wide range of activities right in order to ensure that the team is successful.

Young people look for variety, challenge and opportunity as well as reward in their future lives, and a business life offers all of this and more. There is always some different facet of business skill which will demand and develop the latent interests and abilities of each and every person for, as this book shows, business and its needs are as broad as life itself. I congratulate UI for producing so useful an addition to the field of education/ business partnerships.

Perhaps the biggest misconception of all is that business is bureaucratic and unchallenging. If it is, it doesn't last long in today's fast moving world. Business is about change – constantly doing things better – every day producing more and better things needed by people, for less. I hope this book will help to further a greater appreciation of this and will enable and encourage more of you to look at what we have to offer for the future. We need you and you, whether you wish to follow a business career or not, need us.

Sir John Harvey-Jones
Industrialist

Introduction

Introduction: do we still need manufacturing?

The traditional perception that many people have of manufacturing industry in Britain is of soot-blackened factories belching out their smoke onto grimy, blighted landscapes. It is an image that has proved remarkably persistent. Yet the 'smoke stack' industries of the Industrial Revolution, from which this view of industry is derived, have long since ceased to dominate Britain's skyline. The image has about as much relevance to industry today as horses and carts have to modern farming.

At the start of the Industrial Revolution in Britain, which took place around 1750, 80 per cent of the workforce was employed in agriculture. During the early stages of industrialisation, the balance shifted as the majority of workers moved away from the land to find jobs in the new mines and factories that were growing up on the coalfields. The numbers working in manufacturing then began to show a marked decline during the early part of this century. By 1955, manufacturing accounted for 42 per cent of people employed. This figure has since fallen even further, to 20.3 per cent in 1994. In contrast, the **service sector** now accounts for 73.3 per cent of those employed.

Following the same pattern as other developed nations with a long history of industrialisation, Britain's economy has shown a decrease in manufacturing industries and a corresponding increase in service industries. Manufacturing industries provide 22.6 per cent of the country's **Gross Domestic Product** or **GDP** (which is the total value of all the goods and services produced). Service industries, on the other hand, now account for 65.3 per cent of GDP. Is this decline in manufacturing's share of GDP a cause for concern or is it in fact an indication of progress? After all, as countries advance they tend to shift away from a primarily agricultural economy to one which is based on manufacturing. Perhaps a service-based economy is simply the next stage of advancement?

Sony's chairman, Akio Morita, has warned that far from being the sign of a maturing economy and therefore something to be encouraged, this is a destructive trend. 'For in the long run an economy that has lost its manufacturing base has lost its vital centre. A service-based economy has no engine to drive it.' He went on to add that, 'When manufacturing prospers, all industries connected with it prosper – not only are more components, parts and salesmen needed, but more accountants, more dentists, more petrol stations, more supermarkets and more schools.' Service industries cannot, therefore, flourish in isolation – they depend on manufacturing to support them.

Manufacturing industries, in turn, rely on a network of service industries within the key areas of banking and finance, law, accountancy and insurance. The role of the financial services sector is particularly important. For example, the Standard Life Assurance Company, one of the largest investors in the UK Stock Market, invest over £50 million pounds in a typical working week. Clearly, then, the contribution made by companies like Standard Life, in providing industries with the funds needed for growth and development, is central to the health of the economy.

Up until the mid-1980s, it was widely assumed that services such as tourism could eventually take over from manufacturing as some kind of 'higher' business activity. However, as Lord Weinstock, managing director of GEC, pointed out at the time in a speech on overseas trade, 'What will the service industries be servicing when no wealth is actually being produced? We will supply the Changing of the Guard and the Beefeaters around the Tower of London. We will become a curiosity. I do not think this is what Britain is all about.' In the event, as the decade drew to a close and growth in the service sector slowed to a halt, it became abundantly clear that service industries alone did not hold the key to Britain's future prosperity.

In any case, there was a growing realisation that manufacturing industries had a more important role to play than services because of the potentially greater value that they could add to the economy. Manufactured goods have **value added** in the course of the production process as they are converted from a raw material to a finished product. This is why furniture, for example, costs far more than the timber it is made from. The value added when goods are manufactured is far greater than when services are provided – one calculation estimates that £3 of services are needed to counterbalance the loss of every £1 of manufactured goods.

A further advantage of manufacturing is highlighted by Sir Trevor Holdsworth, the former chairman of GKN, in a talk given recently at London's Royal Society of Arts. In describing the crucial role played by manufacturing in providing goods for export, he points out that goods worth over £121 billion are exported every year from Britain. Manufactured goods actually account for more than 82 per cent of Britain's exports. 'Only 23 per cent of services are capable of being traded overseas. Manufactured goods provide us with a greater export contribution than banking, insurance and oil put together.' In fact, Britain is still the fourth biggest exporter of manufactured goods in the world.

Producing as many manufactured goods as possible in Britain also helps to reduce our dependence on imports. In the heady days of the Industrial Revolution, Britain was the 'workshop of the world'. However, imports of manufactured goods exceeded exports for the first time in our industrial history in 1983. The need to reverse this trend of **import penetration** gains even greater significance when it is realised that we now import a third of all the manufactured goods we need, spending almost £2 billion a week in the process. How many more jobs would there be and how much more wealth would be created if these imported goods were made in Britain?

The role of manufacturing in the 1990s

The situation facing manufacturing industry today is inevitably a reflection of the events that occurred during the previous decade. Throughout the 1980s, Britain's traditional role as a manufacturing nation came under threat from those who saw the growth in the then booming services sector as the key to our future prosperity. In fact, there was a strong body of opinion which believed that manufacturing no longer played an important role within the economy.

It was a viewpoint coloured by the enormous revenues being generated by North Sea oil and gas at that time. In 1985, when their contribution to trade was at its peak, North Sea oil and gas accounted for nearly a quarter of all exports. According to Michael Porter in his book, *The Competitive Advantage of Nations*, 'North Sea oil and gas have provided an enormous windfall to the British economy and maintained export volume. If anything, however, the discovery of oil has been more of a disadvantage than an advantage because it delayed important policy shifts to revitalise the economy.' Given that North sea oil and gas enabled the country to build up huge trade surpluses almost effortlessly (producing a total trade surplus of £23 billion between 1980 and 1985), it is possible to see how the health of manufacturing came to be relegated to a back-seat position.

The early part of the 1980s were of course over-shadowed by the recession of 1980/81 which wiped out many thousands of companies and about a quarter of the 7 million jobs in the manufacturing sector. The late 1980s are remembered mainly for the consumer boom and wild price escalation in the housing and commercial property markets. Yet this was also the time when, after years in the slow lane, manufacturers in the UK appeared to be closing the gap with their main competitors in other industrial nations.

However, by the early 1990s, all hopes of sustaining the so-called 'productivity miracle' evaporated as manufacturing industry struggled to survive in the throes of the worst recession since the depression of the 1930s. It was a recession which saw GDP fall by 4 per cent and unemployment rise by 1.4 million up to April 1993. The prolonged period of high interest rates in the wake of the consumer boom caused a huge backlash of job losses and company liquidations. It will be some time before industry recovers fully from the lack of investment in capital plant and equipment, research and development, apprenticeships and staff training – all of which suffered heavily from the cutbacks imposed during the recession.

More recently, there have been signs that the UK economy has emerged from recession. Manufacturing productivity, which had improved by only 0.9 per cent in 1990 and 0.5 per cent in 1991 increased by 5 per cent in 1992. The need to rejuvenate our manufacturing base is now widely recognised as an official priority. We still need manufacturing because it is a crucial contributor to GDP and is also the best way of adding value and strengthening the economy.

The pattern of government spending within the UK is typical of developed countries with a high GDP. It is important to remember that this level of expenditure could not be sustained if the wealth creating sector did not provide the necessary revenue in the first place.

The revenue distributed by the government is raised through personal taxation and the Corporation Tax paid by companies. If large numbers of companies go out of business, the Treasury would find it difficult to pay for these essential services with a resulting drop in the standard of service provided.

The level of government spending is therefore influenced by the health of the economy which is in turn a reflection of the profitability of the companies.

CASE STUDY

Standard Life – providing a secure future

Along with manufacturing industries, service industries also have an important role to play in generating wealth for the economy. The Standard Life Assurance Company provides one of the clearest illustrations of the contribution that is made by service sector industries. The company was founded in Edinburgh back in.1825. Within a short time, branches had been set up in the far corners of the world from Brazil and the West Indies to China and India. By the turn of the century, this rapid expansion had made 'The Standard', as it came to be affectionately known, the most popular life assurance company in the world.

In later years, the company decided to consolidate its operations within the UK, Ireland and Canada. More recently, the acquisition of a Spanish life assurance company provided the first foothold in an expansion programme geared to tapping the wider opportunities created by the opening up of the Single European Market.

Standard Life is now one of the largest life assurance companies in the world with a staff of 7,500 and assets of over £35 billion under management. It is one of the major investors in the UK equity market with a huge investment allocation of over £50 million a week. In addition, it looks after the life and pension needs of over 2 million policyholders. So how has the company fared over the years in meeting these responsibilities?

In fact, Standard Life has consistently achieved an excellent record in terms of investment performance, financial security and returns to shareholders. It has the distinction of being the only company to have always been ranked amongst the four top-performing companies since *The Economist* first began running performance surveys of the industry in 1950. Most importantly, the company has been awarded the coveted 'Triple A' rating for financial strength by the top US credit-rating agencies. The strong performance of a long-established company like Standard Life is obviously vital to the creation of a healthy economy.

In which areas does Britain have a strong competitive advantage?

Michael Porter in his book, *The Competitive Advantage of Nations*, has compared the industrial nations of the world in order to discover where their strengths and weaknesses lie in relation to competitive advantage. In Britain's case, he identified a range of areas where a strong national competitive position has been achieved.

'The largest concentration of British competitive advantage is in consumer packaged goods, including alcoholic drinks, food, personal products and household products. Another consumer-related cluster is in the area of household furnishing. Related to these is a strong position in many areas of consumer goods retailing.

Another important cluster is in financial or financially-related services such as insurance, auctioneering, trading, money management and international legal services. Looming large in export volume are petroleum and chemicals, including paint. Significant clusters are also present in pharmaceuticals, computing equipment and software, entertainment and leisure products, printed office products, defence, motors and engines and textiles (largely fibres).'

It is encouraging for Britain's future prosperity that so many of these industries with a strong competitive position are in the fast growing 'sunrise' industries rather than the declining 'sunset' industries. Unlike the *heavy* industries which are important in the early stages of the Industrial Revolution, such as metal working, textiles, shipbuilding and coal mining, the *light* or sunrise industries which have developed in this country are growing. They include motor vehicles, electronics, aerospace, pharmaceuticals and consumer goods industries in general.

It is on these high-tech, high value-added industries, with their greater profit potential and export potential, that Britain's hopes for the future are pinned.

Many of the sunrise industries also have the important advantage of being knowledge rather than labour-intensive. According to Professor Douglas McWilliams, the former chief economic adviser at the Confederation of British Industry (CBI), 'Low-skilled production is increasingly migrating to developing economies with rock-bottom labour costs, particularly those around the Pacific Rim. The only way we can remain competitive is by constantly up-skilling the manufacturing base. Companies must make themselves more innovative and high tech in order to compensate for the jobs that will inevitably disappear overseas.' In other words, those firms that do remain labour-intensive are likely to face an uncertain future.

What is the key to greater competitiveness?

Competing on a world-beating scale involves being successful in a number of key interrelated areas. The first step is undoubtedly to develop a strong **consumer focus**, which means listening to what customers want in order to respond, or better still anticipate their needs. It follows from this that firms need to introduce a constant stream of innovative new products in order to stay ahead of the competition. A high degree of innovation does, of course, require a large scale commitment of funds for **research and development**.

In addition, the selective use of **automation** can be beneficial, though large scale automation is not necessarily appropriate to all firms and all industries. In any case, there is always the danger that if the production processes are not streamlined and re-organised beforehand, the automation will merely speed up the existing problems, not solve them. Nevertheless, automation can, if it is well planned, increase the rate of production, improve reliability and reduce the time it takes to introduce new products onto the market.

However, the costs of developing innovative new products, particularly in high technology industries, and of installing automation and robotics are so great that there is generally a long payback period before the investment can be expected to yield any returns. Given that it is vital to the long-term competitiveness of industry for firms to invest in the future, this suggests that City financiers will have to be more prepared to lend 'patient money'. Unlike their Japanese and German counterparts, they have tended to be preoccupied with short-term profits at the expense of long-term investment.

Yet even if firms manage to improve their performance in all these areas, it will count for nothing if in the final analysis the quality of their products does not match that of their competitors. So what are the standards required for competing on a global scale?

British firms would certainly be far too vulnerable if they attempted to compete in world markets by virtue of their lower prices. In any case, studies have shown that buying decisions are rarely made on the basis of price alone. Invariably, products are bought because they are regarded as being of a superior quality, in terms both of their design and performance and of the standards of customer service offered.

Competitiveness today depends on much more than low prices. It is increasingly dependent on a whole range of non-price factors, including good design, technological innovation, reliability, delivery on time and after-sales service; in short, on quality. Many British firms have managed to transform their fortunes in recent years, through having made a concerted effort to get all these aspects of quality right.

This does not mean, however, that they can now afford to sit back. What is certain is that the targets for world class manufacturing are constantly expanding. As ever, it appears that the Japanese are setting the standards to beat. Simon Caulkin points out in an article in *Management Today* that, 'Already the Japanese are beginning to talk of 'taken for granted' quality and product features, and are moving on to compete by 'surprising' and 'delighting' customers . . . quality and customer satisfaction are 1980s concepts. The aim now must be not just to meet customer needs but to exceed them.'

Whilst the newly industrialised low-wage economies such as Hong Kong and Taiwan account for some of the competition facing British firms, there is no doubt that Japan has become the major force to be reckoned with.

Japanese firms in Britain: the ultimate challenge?

The first Japanese company to establish a plant in the UK was YKK, the zip manufacturer, in 1971. This was followed in 1974 by the Sony television factory at Bridgend in South Wales. Since then, an estimated 120 Japanese companies have established manufacturing plants here, and over the past five years they have trebled their workforce to nearly 30,000. This is quite apart from the Japanese companies operating within the services sector. In fact, more than half of the total Japanese investment in Britain is actually in finance and insurance industries. Overall, Japanese investment in Britain is the highest in Europe. Wales is attracting the most investment, with the north and the south-east the next most popular regions.

So why is the UK proving so attractive to Japanese companies?

- The UK possesses a well-equipped transport infrastructure, with the Channel Tunnel offering even greater potential.
- It has relatively low wage rates for the skilled and semi-skilled workers needed in Japanese factories, which tend to be predominantly assembly plants. Unit labour costs are 20 per cent below the average for Europe and well below those of the high wage economies of countries like the Netherlands and West Germany.
- There is a changing industrial relations climate, with a new willingness amongst unions to negotiate strike-free, single union contracts with employers.
- There are the obvious advantages of operating in a country that speaks the international business language. English is, in fact, the first foreign language taught in Japan.
- The attitude of the UK Government towards Japanese companies is favourable. Investment is encouraged because it is regarded as a means of helping to reduce unemployment levels.
- Companies can obtain grants and subsidies and a range of other perks, such as the option of making deferred payments for loans and taxes, by locating in the economically depressed development areas.
- Finally, and some would say most importantly, Japanese companies see Britain as an ideal 'internal bridgehead' for access to Europe.

All the signs suggest that the pace of Japanese expansion in Britain is increasing. This has given rise to renewed fears that the benefits to the UK economy are minimal, as Japanese manufacturing investment has up to now consisted mainly of 'screwdriver' plants which merely assemble components imported from Japan.

A Market Intelligence (MINTEL) report, published in November 1990, describes the position within the UK car industry. 'Japanese imports of vehicles into Europe have been limited by quota through bilateral trade agreements with individual European countries. . . . To overcome this barrier, Nissan, Honda and Toyota are establishing production facilities in the UK, from which to supply the rest of the European market and at the same time overcome national import restrictions. . . . The potential outlook for the future of UK based car production is that, by the latter half of the 1990s, one third of all UK based production could be Japanese.'

Some regard the influx of Japanese firms as a 'shot in the arm' for British industry, whilst others question the wisdom of encouraging aggressive competitors to locate within the home market. In addition, the fact that they generally operate from new, purpose-built factories with all the latest production technology (subsidised by government loans in the development areas), gives them a significant advantage in terms of lower start-up and operating costs. In contrast, British manufacturers, particularly in the long established mature industries, often have to contend with older buildings and machinery, and are thus vulnerable to competition on the basis of cost.

Critics also claim that by substituting Japanese designed and manufactured products for home produced ones, often in order to avoid the high research and development costs, some British firms stand to lose the skills and expertise needed to create, design, engineer and produce new products.

Barrie James in his book, *The Trojan Horse*, makes the point that, 'Rover's partnership with Honda provides the former with access to badly needed new models and Honda's expertise at a fraction of the cost of developing the internal capability, but the real cost has been Rover's dependence on Honda.' And once these creative skills are lost they are almost impossible to recreate. What will be the impact on Britain's long term competitiveness if the skills needed to create high value-added products are lost?

Some Japanese multinationals such as Canon, Nissan and Sharp are now responding to pleas from industry that they should set up research and development operations in Britain in order to boost the quality of their investment away from 'screwdriver' assembly into high value added activities.

In addition, many Japanese companies are committed to increasing the amount of components they buy from Britain, though they argue that this is difficult because of the quality, cost and delivery problems they face from British suppliers. However, the Sony plant at Bridgend, for instance, now obtains over 90 per cent of its components locally. In the long-term, the demanding requirements set by Japanese firms are likely to influence British suppliers to improve their standards of quality and reliability.

Some observers argue that British manufacturing firms are now facing the 'ultimate challenge'. The next few decades will determine whether Japanese investment in Britain is viewed by future generations as a beneficial development or whether it will come to be known as the proverbial Trojan horse.

The structure of industry

Britain has a **mixed economy**, which means that some firms operate on a free enterprise basis, whilst others are under direct state control – the **nationalised** industries. Many of these have been **privatised** in recent years, such as BT and British Gas. There are three sectors within the economy:

- The **primary** sector – where resources are extracted from the ground, e.g. mining, quarrying, drilling for oil, farming and fishing.
- The **secondary** sector – where these primary products or raw materials are used to manufacture goods, e.g. electronics, steel, cars, clothes etc.
- The **tertiary** sector – where services are provided, e.g. banking, retailing, advertising, tourism and so on, and also public services such as health, education, defence etc.

Businesses in the private sector vary in size from small start-up firms to large multinational corporations. Yet, despite this tremendous diversity in organisation there are, in fact, only three different legal forms which they can take – sole trader, partnership and limited company. These tend, in general, to be associated with the stage of development reached by the firm, with most small start-up firms operating as sole traders and larger, established companies trading as limited companies.

Most **entrepreneurs** operate as **sole traders** initially, because this is the easiest way to start up, as no complicated legal formalities are involved. By definition, entrepreneurs are undertaking a risk in a new commercial venture. They have **unlimited liability**, which means that if the business fails they may have to sell their home and personal possessions to pay outstanding bills. This is balanced by the fact that they keep any profits made and have complete freedom in decision making.

In time, sole traders may decide to form a **partnership** – a decision that is usually taken in order to raise more capital for expansion. In order to avoid disagreements, most partners draw up a formal **partnership agreement**, to include details on, for instance, how much capital is contributed by each partner and the ratio in which profits and losses are to be shared.

As the business develops, further capital for expansion can be obtained by becoming a company and selling shares. Shares in **private limited companies** are not freely available to the general public and can only be transferred with the agreement of the directors. Shares in **public limited companies**, on the other hand, *can* be sold to the general public, though companies have to meet the stringent financial requirements of the Stock Exchange and have a share capital of at least $50,000 before they can 'go public'.

In becoming a company the business acquires a legal identity, which is separate from the shareholders and means that, for instance, it can be sued. Shareholders also have **limited liability** – if the business fails they are only responsible for an amount equivalent to their original investment. For this reason, a private limited company must have **Ltd** after its name and a public company **Plc** after its name, in order to make it clear to suppliers or anyone else dealing with them, that their liability as companies is limited. When a company is registered at Companies House, a **memorandum of association** is drawn up which provides details such as the company's name and address, how much share capital is to be issued and so on.

The essential differences between these three types of business units are shown in Table 1.1.

Table 1.1 *Types of business unit*

	Sole Traders	*Partnership*	*Limited Company*
Owners	One owner	Two to 20 owners – can be more in partnerships of solicitors and accountants etc.	Minimum of two shareholders
Management decisions	Owner	Partners	Board of directors elected by shareholders
Provision of funds	Owner's funds	Partners' funds contributed in amounts laid down in partnership agreement	Shareholders funds up to maximum amount stated in memorandum – for public limited company the minimum share capital to be **quoted** on the Stock Exchange is £50,000
Financial risk	Owner has unlimited liability	Partners have unlimited liability	Liability is limited to value of shareholding
Allocation of profiits	Owner takes profits	Partners agree on how profit should be paid	Directors decide how much profit should be paid as dividends on shares and how much is ploughed back as investment
Duration	Ends on death of owner	Can be dissolved according to terms stated in partnership agreement, or ends on death of partner	Ends on liquidation, when assets are sold off and the company is legally wound up

Marketing and Sales

Introduction: what is marketing?

Firms do not have a choice about whether or not to carry out any marketing. Every organisation markets itself, if only through the kinds of products and services it offers and the standard of its customer service. The only choice is between whether the marketing is done haphazardly or whether it is done systematically, through co-ordinating every aspect of the **marketing effort**. Marketing is often confused with selling or advertising. While both of these functions are involved, the total marketing effort also includes assessing customer needs and carrying out market research, together with the development of the product and its pricing, promotion and distribution.

The key task for any business is to get its marketing right, but this also means the company must be good at everything else from research and development to manufacturing and from quality control to financial control. Marketing does not function in isolation from other departments, but permeates the company. It is no more the exclusive responsibility of the marketing department than profitability is solely the responsibility of the finance department.

According to the Chartered Institute of Marketing, it is 'the management process responsible for identifying, anticipating and satisfying customer requirements profitably'. This means getting the right product or service in the right place at the right time, in the right quantities and at the right price, to ensure enough profit for the company.

WHY HAS MARKETING INCREASED?

In the early days of industrialisation, output could not keep pace with demand. Industries therefore operated in a **sellers' market**. This resulted in a **production orientation**, where firms concentrated on producing the goods they wanted to make. The disregard for consumer preferences at the time is summed up by the 'take it or leave it' attitude of Henry Ford. His comment, 'They can have any colour they like, as long as it's black', reveals an offhand approach which can largely be explained by the lack of competition – Ford had a 50 per cent share of the American car market in the 1920s.

However, particularly since the Second World War, firms have had to adopt a **marketing orientation**, in order to survive in today's fiercely competitive markets. Industries now operate in a **buyer's market**, where consumers can choose what they want to buy from the immense variety of products and services on offer. Firms have to concentrate on producing the goods the market wants, rather than the ones they happen to make.

This changing orientation applies also to overseas markets. Firms can no longer presume, in these days of global competition, that the world will beat a path to their door. Competition has intensified as the open market in Europe presents a tremendous marketing opportunity, but also poses a huge potential threat for the unprepared firm.

What do people need and want?

Marketing starts with finding out what motivates customers to buy a particular product or service. As Peter Drucker, the American management expert, emphasises, 'The aim of marketing is to make selling superfluous. The aim is to know and understand the customer so well that the product or service sells itself.'

This means identifying the customer's **needs** and **wants**. Philip Kotler, in his book *Principles of Marketing*, defines needs as 'a state of felt deprivation in a person' while wants are 'needs as shaped by our culture and personality'. In other words, all people need to eat, but one person may want beefburger and chips while another might want salmon and caviar. Wants only become **demand** when people have the resources to acquire what they want. For example, many people might want a Rolls Royce but only a few can afford to buy one, so the demand for Rolls Royces is small.

American psychologist AH Maslow has argued that people have different levels of needs. They seek to satisfy lower level needs, such as those for food, drink, shelter and safety, before trying to fulfil their higher order needs, for things such as social acceptance, status and self-fulfilment. However, people do respond differently in the way they satisfy a particular need according to their attitudes, social values and so on. The implication, therefore, is that consumers do not simply buy a product or service – they buy *solutions* to their perceived problems or needs. If the marketing effort is to be successful, it must emphasise the *benefits* consumers will gain by using the product or service.

Maslow's hierarchy of needs

In fact, what people want is usually far more than they need. In buying an expensive house, the successful person is making a statement about his or her status and position in society rather than just buying a shelter from the elements. Which marketing campaign for expensive houses is likely to be most effective – one which emphasises how structurally sound the houses are, or one which portrays a comfortable lifestyle with glamorous people in elegant room settings? In the same way most campaigns are cleverly aimed at subtly exploiting the often subconscious wants which influence people's buying decisions.

As most consumers' needs and wants are already being catered for, much effort also goes into creating new needs and wants by developing innovative products. Once introduced onto the market, these exploit wants which were **latent** and not expressed until the new product became available. How many of you knew you wanted a personal stereo until Sony actually brought out their Walkman?

Innovative products can therefore stimulate new consumer wants, but what about the reverse situation? Can new consumer wants stimulate innovative products being developed? In fact, this has already happened. For instance, in the plastics and synthetic fibre industries, the marketing people tell the researchers what properties they need and the researchers then design those materials. The implications of the fact that we can now 'innovate to order' are far reaching.

Discussion points

1   Do advertisers encourage materialism by constantly exploiting people's needs and wants?
2   What are some of the products and services which are advertised to exploit each level of Maslow's hierarchy of needs?

Is market research essential?

Carrying out detailed market research, whether it concerns products and services aimed at domestic consumers or those aimed at industrial consumers, is the first step in any effective marketing campaign. Market research provides information which is sufficiently objective to form a basis for decision making. Firms generally start by looking at the information already available within their own company, from sales and account records and so on. These can show:

* Which products are most profitable.
* Whether sales fall into a pattern by type of product, by customer, by geographical area or by size of order.
* Whether the company is becoming too dependent on a few customers or products.
* Which customer accounts are most profitable.
* What proportion of sales quotations result in actual orders.

The next step for firms is to consult other sources of information which have already been published, such as government publications, media reports, newspapers and journals. These can show:

* Whether the total market for a particular product or service is growing, static or declining.
* What changes are taking place in the market.
* Who the main competitors are.

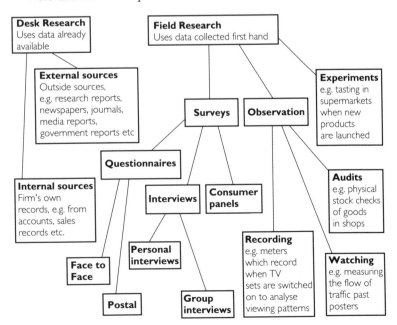

Quantitative methods of market research

If neither of these forms of **desk research** provides all the information required, the firm may then decide some **field research** is needed, which it can either do itself or commission a market research agency to carry out.

In any case, only a **sample** of people would be researched. It is not practical or even necessary to contact every person in the potential market! The group of people can be a **random sample** picked from the electoral registers, telephone directories and so on, or a **stratified sample**, where a representative cross-section of the population in terms of factors such as age, sex, income etc. is researched. Alternatively, interviewers may be given a **quota**. If they are conducting street interviews this means that they can choose whom to interview, providing they survey a certain number of people from, for example, each age group.

Once the size and type of sample has been chosen firms can then carry out **quantitative research** to provide answers to such questions as *how many* people buy their product. They can also carry out **qualitative research** by means of group discussions and in-depth interviews, to establish such factors as *who* buys their products and *why*.

Market research cannot, of course, eliminate business risk, but it can greatly reduce the guesswork element.

Potentially disastrous situations can thus be avoided, such as when a huge capital investment is made in a product for which there is no demand. This sounds unlikely, yet even highly innovative products have been known to fail because they are sold in a market which has not been correctly identified. The Sinclair C5 is a good example.

Discussion point

Could the Sinclair C5 have succeeded in other markets? (consider golf trollies etc.)

Stages of market research

Decide on purpose of market research, what information needs to be obtained and what action will be taken as a result of research findings.

↓

Decide on most appropriate market research method(s) taking into account time and budget constraints.

↓

Decide on size and composition of sample to be studied, in line with the objectives of the research.

↓

Carry out research using appropriate methods.

↓

Gather and analyse data from research.

↓

Present findings in a report. Summarise main findings, draw conclusions and make recommendations on what actions need to be taken as a result of research.

CASE STUDY

The launch of Wispa – hit or hype?

In the beginning it was known only as P46 – just one of many potential new products developed by Cadbury's research and development department. The account of how this new chocolate aerated bar became one of the most successful launches of the decade is one of elaborate marketing strategies, designed to maintain the element of surprise at all costs.

The total UK confectionery market is worth a huge £3.7 billion, with chocolate accounting for 71 per cent of that amount. Cadbury has a 30 per cent share of this market today, though at the time of the launch its position was declining slightly relative to its major competitors.

Cadbury needed to introduce a successful new product, though picking future winners is not so easy in the notoriously fickle confectionery market, as shown by brands such as Banjo, Cabana, Nutty and Drifter, which have all faded from the market. However, pre-launch market research indicated the aerated bar was liked. More importantly, research established that the brand was perceived as unique, which was an important consideration as copycat brands or 'me too' products often do not survive for long. On the basis of these research findings, the decision was taken to build a new pilot production plant at Bournville.

Cadbury's Wispa bar pack

The main problem for Young & Rubicam, the agency running the advertising campaign for Wispa, was how to overcome the consumer's belief that chocolate was just chocolate. Eventually, the 'Duos' campaign was designed, with a central theme focused on the conversion of a cynic who finds it hard to believe, until he tastes Wispa, that chocolate can be so indescribably different. Cadbury chose TV as the only medium with enough impact to introduce the heavy trial the product needed. The only back-up promotion was a 5p coupon in the local press.

As with any new product, Wispa was initially marketed in a **test region** to assess reaction before major investment was made in a national launch. Tyne Tees was chosen because it is a fairly neat, self-contained TV region, representing 5 per cent of total UK spending power.

Wispa's arrival was hinted at in the **teaser advertisements** on TV, put out for a week before the actual launch. Young & Rubicam's campaign obviously hit the target, as consumer reaction was unprecedented. TV advertising had to be stopped after only three weeks as the pilot plant could not cope with the demand. There were reports of black-market dealing, shopkeepers rationing supplies and a serious fight over the last two boxes in one cash-and-carry store.

In an elaborate ploy to persuade the competition that Wispa had flopped, the company withdrew it, putting their resources into a secret £12 million programme to build a major computerised plant geared to coping with this level of demand. An elaborate veil of secrecy was drawn around the project in order to stop news leaking out to competitors and damaging the relaunch. Machinery was built from an assortment of individually bought parts so that manufacturers of factory plant were not alerted. Advertising was booked under other brand names and switched to Wispa at the last moment. Boxes of bars left the factory in black polythene bags in unmarked vans to be held in special cold stores. Retailers were only informed by letters timed to arrive on the first day of the relaunch.

In the meantime, Rowntree had brought out Aero – their new chunky aerated bar, which was an instant success. This meant Wispa's relaunch had to be supported by intensive advertising, costing a hefty £6m. **Tracking study** results had proved that the 'Duos' campaign was very effective, so it was used again, this time with stars from *Hi de Hi*, *Yes Minister* and *It Ain't Half Hot Mum*, together with poster and bus-side advertising. The relaunch started in Tyne Tees and with military precision the national **roll out** was extended to other regions, breaking sales records as it went. One shop in Newcastle sold 36,000 bars in two days!

Competitors were sceptical, claiming that part of Wispa's success was achieved at the expense of some of Cadbury's other products like Flake and that sales dropped after the excitement of the initial launch. However, subsequent market research suggests product awareness is good and that the level of repeat purchases is high, indicating **brand loyalties** forming. Wispa is still one of the Top Ten Countlines along with the old favourites Kit Kat, Mars and Twix, and is a good example of how a new brand can expand the total market. 'Hit or hype', industry leaders are agreed the confectionery business has never seen anything quite like it before.

How is the market divided up?

The pattern of replies drawn from market research provides clues as to the kinds of people who are likely to buy that product or service. Several distinct groups of customers are revealed who make up sections or **segments** within the total market. Once the characteristics and buying behaviour of these groups is known, marketing can then be directed at the particular segments or **target groups** which have been identified as containing the most potential customers.

The firm can then establish its **market position** by concentrating the marketing effort on the particular segment which is likely to yield the highest sales for its products or services. The advantage of identifying target groups is that the sales effort can be directed by means of a 'rifle shot' approach at the people who are most likely to buy. This is far more effective than aiming the sales effort at the market in general, as in the scattered 'shotgun' approach.

Market segments are divided up on the basis of demographic factors, such as age, sex and geographical area, and also on consumers' income, occupation and ethnic group. Segments can also be divided up in terms of many other factors, such as whether people are heavy or light users of the product or service.

One of the most common ways of defining market segments is by **socioeconomic group (SEG)**. Table 2.1 illustrates this. People within the same SEG tend to show certain similarities in their expectations, values and behaviour compared with members of other groups. However, this is a very general classification and some overlapping does occur. For example, some people from the lower SEGs may earn more than those from higher SEGs.

The markets for most **fast-moving consumer goods** tend to be highly segmented, for example, soaps, shampoos, cigarettes, biscuits etc. Some companies try to offer a range of products which exploits all segments. However, they need to be aware of the danger of **fragmentation**. This occurs if they try to cater for too many segments, when each segment becomes so small that very little profit is generated.

Table 2.1 *JICNARS social grade definitions*

Social grade	Social status	Occupation
A	Upper middle class	Higher managerial, administrative, or professional
B	Middle class	Intermediate managerial, administrative or professional
C1	Lower middle class	Supervisory or clerical, and junior managerial, administrative or professional
C2	Skilled working class	Skilled manual workers
D	Working class	Semi-skilled and unskilled manual workers
E	Those at lowest level of subsistence	State pensioners or widows (no other earner), casual or lowest-grade workers

Source: *JICNARS National Readership Survey*

Small firms generally find it easier to break into a specific segment of a wider market. This enables them to survive by concentrating on supplying a specialised product or service, rather than trying to compete with bigger firms who have cornered the mass market. This strategy of identifying a specialist segment at which marketing can be targeted is called **niche marketing**.

Markets should, however, always be segmented on the basis of what customers want or need, not on the basis of the products they buy. This is an important distinction. Firms who think they are just in the business of making slide rules and concentrate all their efforts on improving their slide rules are in danger of going out of business when a firm comes along which makes calculators. They have ignored the fact that what customers actually want is a product that carries out calculations quickly. They do not want a slide rule as such, so if a better product becomes available which does calculations quickly, consumers will buy that instead.

ACTIVITY

Identifying target groups

1 Decide what target group each of the following products or services is aimed at and the needs which are being catered for in each case.

Spray furniture polish	TV rental shops
Building society accounts	'Oh Boy!' magazine
Ford Fiestas	Polyfilla
Ready meals	Life insurance
Rolls Royces	Season tickets
	'Financial Times'

2 What are some of the market segments for the following products or services?

Shampoos (e.g., normal, dry, greasy, permed, dandruff, frequent wash, baby shampoo etc.)	
Breakfast cereals	
Package holidays	
CDs	Cars
Cheap Day returns	Watches

Who are a firm's main customers?

In many cases, it is common to find that 20 per cent of customers account for 80 per cent of sales. This is known as the 80/20 Rule or **Pareto Effect**.

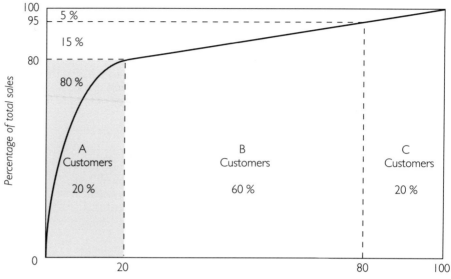

The Pareto Effect

The diagram shows the typical ratio of sales to customer groups found in the Pareto Effect. The A group constitutes 20 per cent of customers and accounts for 80 per cent of total sales. The B group constitutes 60 per cent of customers and accounts for 15 per cent of sales, whilst the C group makes up 20 per cent of customers, but only accounts for 5 per cent of sales. Clearly, firms that are successful in identifying the A group can make their advertising considerably more effective by targeting these important customers. However, they should not forget that some B or C group customers can become A group customers with good service and attention.

The marketing mix

After considering the market research findings and identifying the market segment it intends to target, the firm then needs to offer a total package to meet the customer's needs and wants. Four key areas are blended to produce the required response in the target audience: product, price, place and promotion. These elements make up the **marketing mix**, or 'offering' to the customer.

The right product

A new product is distinct from a **line extension**, such as a 'new' lemon version of a shampoo. Ideas for new products can come from anywhere – the company's own research and development programme, competitors' products and so on. A constant supply of new ideas or **concepts** is needed, as only a small percentage survives screening and test marketing to be launched nationally.

Sometimes it takes marketing flair to think of a good use for an invention. The highly successful yellow Post-it notes were born when 3M invented an adhesive that had low stickiness but retained its properties after repeated use. It wasn't what they were looking for so it was put on the shelf, until years later when another researcher suggested using it for a notepad with pages that stuck but could be peeled off easily. Post-it notes went on to become one of their best sellers – quite a feat in view of the fact that 3M make about 60,000 different products!

Of course, only a handful of new products ever become winners. One reason many products fail is that they are not distinctive enough. If a new product is to succeed, it should have certain features which make it stand out from the competition, so that it forms a **unique selling proportion (USP)**. In reality, these distinguishing features are often very minor. For instance, all shampoos contain the same basic ingredients. It is only the additives which vary slightly. The differences are more in the way each shampoo is packaged, priced and advertised. Creating a unique identity in this way turns a product into a **brand**, which means it can then be sold for more. A comparison between prices of branded goods and supermarket own-label goods illustrates the point.

Companies can increase their total **market share** by introducing many **brand variants** aimed at different segments of the market. For example, Van den Berghs have done this with their margarine brands, such as Stork, Blue Band, Echo, Flora, Krona etc. However, firms must be careful not to introduce brands with a low profit margin that **cannibalise** market share away from their other products which may be brand leaders with higher profit margins.

THE PRODUCT LIFE CYCLE

Any product will pass through various stages in its **life cycle**, just as humans and animals do, although the time span between when it is first introduced and when it is finally withdrawn from the market varies greatly.

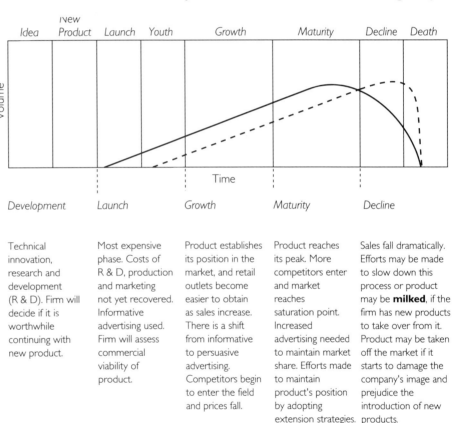

Development	Launch	Growth	Maturity	Decline
Technical innovation, research and development (R & D). Firm will decide if it is worthwhile continuing with new product.	Most expensive phase. Costs of R & D, production and marketing not yet recovered. Informative advertising used. Firm will assess commercial viability of product.	Product establishes its position in the market, and retail outlets become easier to obtain as sales increase. There is a shift from informative to persuasive advertising. Competitors begin to enter the field and prices fall.	Product reaches its peak. More competitors enter and market reaches saturation point. Increased advertising needed to maintain market share. Efforts made to maintain product's position by adopting extension strategies.	Sales fall dramatically. Efforts may be made to slow down this process or product may be **milked**, if the firm has new products to take over from it. Product may be taken off the market if it starts to damage the company's image and prejudice the introduction of new products.

The product life cycle

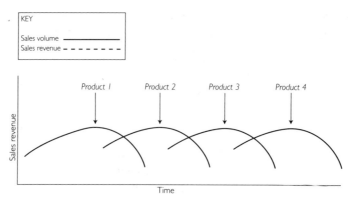

The importance of successive product launches

As products reach maturity in a market which has been fully exploited and has therefore become **saturated**, they start to decline. In some cases, the firm may decide to delay the end by using various **extension strategies**. The product can be given a new lease of life by being repackaged or reformulated. A good example of a long-running brand is Lux soap which is over 80 years old. Its shape, perfume, colour and packaging have changed continuously during that time. Other strategies include finding new uses or markets for the product or bringing out new accessories for it.

Some brands seem to live forever – your parents and maybe even your grandparents will probably remember such classics as Bisto, Oxo, Dettol, Ovaltine, or Coleman's mustard.

Most products do, of course, eventually die. Often this is just because of changing consumer tastes, but increasingly it is because of the rapid pace of technological change. Life cycles are getting shorter and shorter, especially in areas such as the electronics industry. New products become obsolete; often within months rather than years, as each technically more advanced version is brought out.

THE BOSTON MATRIX

A single-product business is very vulnerable in the market place, particularly if it only has a few major customers. Most businesses are therefore **multi-product** firms with a **portfolio** or variety of products, which they try to ensure are all at different stages in their life cycles in order to avoid great fluctuations in profit levels. A well-balanced portfolio also means that the revenue generated by older products can help to nurture new products through their introduction.

The Boston Consulting Group in Massachusetts, USA, have devised a matrix for classifying products in order to analyse whether a firm's product portfolio is well balanced.

The Boston Matrix

CASE STUDY

Oxo – keeping alive a favourite brand

The familiar Oxo cube has been sprinkled into countless soups, casseroles and gravies since it started life as the 'penny cube', back in 1910. In the years since, it has come to be seen as a standard item in most kitchen store cupboards and has become a best selling brand for its makers, Brooke Bond Foods. Literally millions of cubes are sold a day of Original Oxo, Chicken Oxo, Vegetable Oxo and the new international seasoning cube.

However, by the 1980s Brooke Bond Foods were facing the problem that arises sooner or later with any long-established brand. The market was becoming more and more fragmented with products such as packet sauces providing an alternative way of flavouring. At the same time, eating habits were changing – people were eating fewer beef dishes and traditional family meals were becoming less common. These two trends were making it increasingly difficult to expand sales much further. The company had a choice. Should any more be invested in the brand or should it be 'milked' for short-term profits?

In the event, they decided to take the long-term view and began to develop a major new campaign with their advertising agency, J Walter Thompson. The main aim was to make certain that Oxo was seen as being relevant to good cooking in today's family life. Most importantly, the campaign had to maintain usage frequencies and to reinforce the habit of automatically replacing cupboard stocks.

The market research into family life revealed some interesting findings. It showed that what people associated with family life was partly the daily grind – washing, children, being tired, fighting, money, cheek, squabbling, making food, getting them to eat it, noise and lack of sleep! However, people also associated family life with other aspects such as warmth, caring, security, relief and gentleness. Not surprisingly, research showed as well that people were critical of the artificially perfect families typical of the advertising dream, and were far more interested in the families shown in programmes such as *Brookside*. In the light of these findings, the 'Family' campaign created by J Walter Thompson was a complete departure from the stereotyped ideal families usually portrayed in advertising. In fact, their highly acclaimed 'slice of life' adverts created a whole new genre in the industry which has been much copied since.

A large part of the campaign's popularity is without doubt due to the fact that viewers are able to identify with the adverts. They can see aspects of their own day-to-day lives reflected in the stories about the Oxo family. As a result it was voted the most popular TV campaign for four years running in the *TV Times* awards. Most importantly, it has also achieved its objectives of increasing sales and keeping alive a favourite brand.

Scene from one of the current Oxo commercials

CASE STUDY

*Lucozade – a
strategy for
revival*

When SmithKline Beecham first decided to change the marketing strategy for their well-established Lucozade brand, they expected that sales would increase. Little did they realise, however, that Lucozade would soon become the third largest selling carbonated drink in the UK (after Coca Cola and Pepsi Cola) with sales accelerating from a mere £15 million in 1980 to a massive £145 million by 1994. So how did this transformation come about?

Lucozade is, in fact, a classic example of a product which, through the use of extension strategies – the development of a successful advertising campaign and of new packaging – has increased its sales dramatically. Through being positioned on a different platform in the market, the product has been given a dramatic new lease of life.

Lucozade was introduced back in 1927. By the early 1980s it had reached maturity in its life cycle and might well, after such a long life, have seemed to be heading towards an honourable retirement. Sales levels were static and it had become clear that the brand image was becoming old-fashioned. It was also recognised that the traditional 'Lucozade Aids Recovery' message was restricting consumers perception of Lucozade as being a drink purely for convalescents.

The decision by SmithKline Beecham to change the market positioning of the brand from that of specific convalescent usage to an 'in health' energy drink was a bold move, aimed at exploiting a much wider target market – teenagers and young adults. At the same time, Lucozade was also repackaged in small 'one-shot' bottles and cans, in recognition of the fact that 'on the street' consumption was becoming an increasingly common consumer trend.

The creation of a new advertising campaign was central to the strategy. To this end, a memorable new campaign was developed with their advertising agency, Ogilvy and Mather, which used the outstanding athlete Daley Thompson to endorse Lucozade's new 'high-energy' image. They could not have chosen a better personality. In his own likeable way Daley Thompson symbolised raw energy, sporting achievement and an infectious enthusiasm for life, qualities with which the target market could readily identify.

The new marketing strategy has clearly succeeded in repositioning Lucozade as an energy-giving drink for today's lifestyle. The sales success has prompted the company to introduce a host of product variants – Orange, Lemon and Tropical Barley as well as a Light version. Lucozade Sport, which is the official sports drink of the Premier League, is now promoted by Linford Christie.

Linford Christie promoting Lucozade

The right price

The price of a product or service is another element of the marketing mix, which interacts with the other factors to determine whether or not consumers will buy. The model of demand and supply in the diagram shows how the market works.

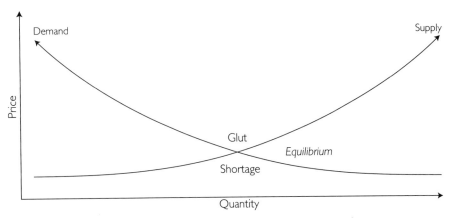

Demand curve - shows more goods are bought when prices are low.
Supply curve - shows suppliers offer more goods when prices are high.
Equilibrium - ideal position for the market, where supply equals demand.
Glut - prices are high and not all goods are sold.
Shortage - prices are low and fewer goods are made.

Supply and demand curve

This overall view of the market provides a simple view of how demand and supply interact. However, a firm's decision as to which pricing strategy to adopt is complicated by many other factors. The pricing strategy will vary according to the stage reached in the product's life cycle and its **position** in the market relative to its competitors. If the product can be differentiated from rival products, perhaps by its good design, or by the quality of the after-sales service offered, then it can be sold for more.

So what pricing strategies might be used?

- **Market penetration** A price is set which is below that of competitors, in order to capture a share of the market. A short-term loss is sometimes accepted, in the hope that the price can be raised after **brand loyalty** has been gained and customers start to reorder the brand by name. The actual products may be priced cheaply in order to encourage customers to buy, but the accessories to go with it may be priced expensively, as with the film for instant cameras.

  However, if prices are pitched too low, customers may become suspicious about quality. Another danger of price cutting is that competitors may retaliate by lowering their prices as well. Firms tend to avoid getting into such a price-cutting war, because the end result is that they all achieve the same market share as they had before, but at a lower price level. A low price strategy may also prove dangerous for products which are expected to have a short life span.
- **Skimming** A high price is set to recover the development costs of new products quickly. Consumers are prepared to pay high prices for products which are innovative and for which there are no substitutes. The Simon computer game, for example, cost £32.95 when it was first introduced, yet only eight months later it was available at £6.95. Similarly, video recorders, calculators, computer games and telephone answering machines all commanded high prices when they were first introduced onto the market. The danger of pricing products too highly is that sales may be lost.
- **Price discrimination** A price is set which varies for different segments of the market – for example, pensioners can get cheap tickets.

- **Competitive pricing** A price is set which is at the same going rate as competitors'. This is common when goods or services provided are very similar and not capable of being differentiated very much, as with home mortgages or petrol.

Having worked out their pricing strategy, firms then need to calculate what price to charge for their goods. The most common pricing method is **cost plus**, which is when the total costs incurred are added together and a suitable percentage **mark-up** added on for profit. In the final analysis, though, the 'right' price should not just be based on the firm's costs. It must relate to the price that sufficient numbers of customers are prepared to pay – that is, the price that the market will bear – which in turn is dependent on how customers perceive the value of the product.

The right place

Having decided on the right product and price, the company has to get the product to the industrial user or final consumer by way of an efficient and cost-effective distribution system.

The traditional **channel of distribution** is from manufacturer to wholesaler to retailer to consumer. Wholesalers, because they are in the middle, have the advantage of **breaking bulk**. This means that retailers can buy in smaller quantities from them, rather than from manufacturers who tend to prefer to make one large delivery.

In recent years this chain has been shortened as many manufacturers have started to sell directly to large retailers who buy in bulk, such as the supermarket chains with their own depots, or to retailers who can carry huge stocks themselves, such as the hypermarkets like Asda. A shorter distribution channel is also used when the product is fragile and handling must be minimised, as with frozen foods, or where the product is bulky, as with furniture. Some manufacturers sell directly to the consumer using mail order.

The method of transport is also important. Cost-effective **physical distribution** can result in significant savings for the company. The choice of transport method is determined by weight, bulk, value and perishability of the goods and by the needs of the company. Road tends to be the most popular as it is the most flexible method, offering a door-to-door service without the restrictions of rail transport. Rail is cheaper for bulky goods and can compete with road over long journeys where the door-to-door factor becomes less critical. Air is used for light, expensive and perishable goods. Sea is used for bulky commodities like oil transported over long distances. In recent years the widespread use of containers has streamlined distribution considerably.

The choice of **distribution outlet** is partly influenced by the image and nature of the product. Expensive perfume would obviously not be sold through supermarkets. Products that have a low unit cost, are purchased frequently and are easily substituted, such as crisps and baked beans, must be widely available or sales are lost.

Retail outlets include supermarkets, hypermarkets, department stores, multiple stores, cooperatives and discount stores. Goods can also be sold by mail order and door-to-door selling. A recent development has been the growth of **franchising**, where the **franchisees** own their own business but the **franchiser** provides the name, products and expertise to run it, with the benefits of economies of scale like bulk buying and national advertising.

The Body Shop group provides a good example of the benefits of franchising where the franchiser is able to expand by functioning, in effect, as a wholesaler. Anita Roddick, 1984's Businesswoman of the Year, has made her Body Shop group something of a retailing legend, with sales accelerating to £195 million in 1994 and numerous applicants waiting for a franchise. With only £4,000 start-up capital, she has managed to expand the business through the franchise route, yet still kept tight control on all the outlets.

The right promotion

Having got the right product and determined the right price the firm must design an effective promotion strategy. There are three aspects of promotion: advertising, sales promotions and public relations.

ADVERTISING

This is the most common type of promotion and one of the earliest forms. As mass production increased in the latter stages of the Industrial Revolution and economies of scale were made, high volume sales were needed, which meant firms had to advertise in order to attract large numbers of customers. As living standards improved still further, encouraging the production of more goods, it was no longer a sellers' market and firms had to compete with each other to persuade customers to buy their product.

Not all advertising is aimed at consumers as the **end users**. Increasingly, advertisers are having to sell to the retailer, which necessitates a different kind of advertising, where the degree of trade acceptability already achieved by the product is emphasised in order to persuade the retailer to stock it.

In the field of industrial marketing, the text of advertisements or **advertising copy** tends to be less emotive and more informative. This is because industrial buying decisions often tend to be made by groups of people rather than individuals, unlike those made by domestic consumers. The decisions also tend to be made in a more formal and methodical way. There is a greater emphasis on advertising in the trade press, trade fairs and exhibitions and on the use of technical brochures.

Commercial television is the most expensive medium to use but is also the most popular because of its effectiveness. Although TV advertising in Britain is only thirty years old, it has produced slogans and catch phrases that have become part of our language, familiar jingles and lasting images. The demands of telling an interesting story in a short space of time are such that it is no accident that one of our most successful directors, Alan Parker of *Bugsy Malone*, *Midnight Express* and *Shoot the Moon* fame, began in films as a director of TV commercials.

Other media that are less expensive include commercial radio, posters, cinema, magazines and journals, newspapers and so on.

ACTIVITY

Identifying types of advertising

Give examples of products and services which are advertised in the following ways:

- **Persuasive** – glamorous images and persuasive language used to encourage consumers to buy. Often called the hard sell.
- **Informative** – used to make consumers aware of the existence and identity of the product. May provide technical information.
- **Corporate** – where a company promotes its name and image rather than an individual product. Benefits overall sales of all products.
- **Generic** – where a group of manufacturers promotes a whole industry or type of product.
- **Competitive** – where companies subtly imply that rival firm's products are inferior to theirs.

Hodder & Stoughton Educational © Permission to photocopy for classroom use only.

SALES PROMOTIONS

These are used to generate short-term increases in sales by encouraging consumers to try the product once, in the hope of generating repeat sales. They include:

- Coupons, vouchers, and percentage reduction (such as 25p off, £1 cash refund, etc.).

- Free samples. These are often used for new products.
- Self-liquidating offers. Goods are offered at cost price for a certain number of tokens or packet tops.
- Free offers, such as free gifts at petrol stations.
- Bargain packs such as '20 per cent extra fee', 'Buy two, get one free' etc.
- Charity promotions. On receipt of a certain number of proofs of purchase, a donation is made to charity.
- Prize promotions and newspaper bingo.

Point-of-sale promotions encourage customers into the shop. A well-known type of price promotion is the use of **loss leaders**, where customers are attracted into the shop by a few products priced cheaply in the hope that they will then buy other products priced normally.

CASE STUDY

Levi 501s – why was denim fading?

The scene is an American laundromat in the 1950s. A young man wearing jeans walks in, calmly takes off his jeans and puts them in the machine. He then sits down amongst the other customers in his boxer shorts and carries on reading while he waits for his jeans to be washed.

This advert, 'Launderette', which was part of the campaign that advertising agency Bartle Bogle Hegarty (BBH) produced for the relaunched Levi 501s, has become a cult classic – one of the most successful adverts of all time. It made the actor, Nick Kamen, an overnight star. In the UK alone, sales rocketed by 800 per cent within the first year. The factory in Scotland where the jeans were stitched together could not meet demand, even by working 18-hour shifts and taking on extra hands. Levi's sold three months' stock of 501s in just three weeks. Shops were besieged by people asking to try on the jeans that 'the bloke in the launderette wears'.

Yet before the decision was taken to relaunch the original 501 classic design, Levi Strauss, who are the world's biggest manufacturer of jeans, were suffering from a serious downturn in the jean market. The main problem was that by the early 1980s, the 16- to 24-year-olds who buy half of all jeans sold had begun to see denim jeans as a tired legacy of their parents' younger years. Sales in the European jeans market slumped from 250 million pairs in 1981 to 150 million pairs in 1985. Levi's reaction to the declining market was to **diversify** their product base. The trouble was that having moved away from jeans into products ranging from socks to flannel shirts, it got to the point where the Levi's brand name was in danger of being diluted.

Something had to be done. Levi's made the bold decision to go back to basics, reverse the diversification and concentrate on selling jeans. The job of designing the European promotion to accompany the relaunch of the 501 design was given to BBH. The objectives of the campaign were to increase the profitability of the company and to lower the age profile of the brand's consumers, which had been creeping up and away from the **core** of the jeans market as the brand's image had worsened. According to Tim Lindsay, the director in charge of the Levi Strauss account at BBH, 'The **creative brief** was to persuade the 15- to 20-year-old males, who represent the core of the jeans market, that 501s were the right look and the only label.' The campaign had to be designed to appeal to this **target market**. The message also had to be clear without the use of speech, as the adverts were to be shown across Europe.

Market research carried out by BBH revealed a growing desire amongst the young for clothes and objects with a genuine heritage. They also uncovered a fascination for a mythical America of the past – 'the America that had produced Dean and Presley, the '57 Chevrolet and Sam Cooke'.

Further research confirmed that the campaign based around the fifties nostalgia theme was liked. Accordingly 'Launderette' and 'Bath' (with actor

James Mardle getting into a bath to shrink his 501s) went on air in December 1985. They were quickly followed by 'Parting' and 'Entrance'. The later commercials, 'Cochrane', 'Refrigerator' and 'Pick up', also invoke the nostalgia theme.

The series of commercials for 501s has won many industry awards, both in the UK and internationally. They have been discussed on twenty-three different TV programmes, thus providing additional free advertising. Most importantly, the campaign achieved its original objectives of returning the company to profitability and of adjusting the brand's **consumer profile** back to the core of the market.

In addition, Levi's **market share** rocketed from 13 per cent to 18 per cent. Competitors did not complain. They also benefited from the rejuvenated jeans market, which expanded from being worth £550 million in 1985 to £800 million in 1987. Sales of other products also increased. The 'golden oldies' which formed the soundtracks of the adverts all got into the UK top ten when re-released. According to trade sources, 'Launderette' also created a major fashion trend, with over two million pairs of boxer shorts being sold in 1986!

Since then, Levi's have cemented their position as market leaders, gaining a 26 per cent share of a market worth £1.11 billion by 1994. The campaign has also gone from strength to strength, with the latest series of advertisements 'Night and Day', 'Procession', 'Tackle' and 'Campfire' capturing the mood and style of modern day America.

'Creek', focusing on a staid Middle American Sunday picnic opens with a Ma, Pa and their two daughters in a horse-drawn buggy. Enjoying a few moments of freedom, as they run through the woods the girls are stopped in their tracks by the sight of a bare-torsoed man bathing in the creek and a pair of trousers drying on a rock in the sun. From their hiding place the girls watch as our hero wades to the shore and it is revealed that he is wearing a pair of original shrink-to-fit Levi's 501s.

Scenes from Levi's advertisement, Creek.

The Single Market – opportunity or threat?

Before the end of December 1992 the vision of a common market in Europe had finally become reality with the uniting of 12 member states to form a huge single market with no internal frontiers – the European Community (EC).

December 1992 was the date laid down for completion of the internal market in the Single European Act of 1987 – a date which marked the official end of a long evolutionary process of integration. In fact, the dream of a united Europe can be traced back as early as 1957, to the signing of the Treaty of Rome. For Britain, the process of integration actually began when we joined the Common Market in 1973. The completion of the Channel Tunnel, which links Britain to the Continental rail networks, has ended our physical isolation from Europe.

Creation of a single market involves the removal of physical, technical and fiscal (tax) barriers, which have long been recognised as the main barriers to the free movement of goods, services, capital and people. In everyday terms this means that the 320 million citizens of the 12 member states will now be able to live, work and travel in Europe as if it were one big country, in much the same way as people do in the USA, for instance.

For some, entry into the single market represents a major step forward, but for others it spells the end of an era as Britain loses the fiercely guarded independence of centuries. So what are the likely long-term benefits and drawbacks of Britain's entry into the single market?

Will it mean, as some have argued, the gradual surrender of our national sovereignty to the 'Eurocrats' of Brussels and Strasbourg? Certainly, there will be an appreciable loss of decision-making power as the majority voting system of the European Parliament may work against the wishes of individual governments, though governments still retain the right of veto in areas of crucial importance to them.

Perhaps this is the price that national governments have to be prepared to pay in order to be part of a European trading bloc which will rival the industrial might of the USA and Japan. Few would disagree that the pooling of resources is essential. At present, the European market is fragmented, where even the largest market – West Germany with 78 million people – is smaller than Japan and considerably smaller than the USA. On its own, each member state could not hope to compete effectively. But with access to an expanded market of 320 million people firms can drive down costs by producing on a larger scale.

Such economies of scale are particularly important in the high technology growth industries where large sums need to be invested in the research and development of innovative new products. According to Philips, the Dutch electronics group, many electronics products today must capture an 8 per cent world market share just to break even on technology development costs.

Clearly, the expanded market brings opportunities by enabling European firms to compete on a world-beating scale. However, it also poses a huge threat for the unprepared firm. As the internal barriers to trade come down, a 'shake out' of the weakest firms will inevitably follow, especially in those industries which have previously been protected from outside competition by their governments.

In addition, a high degree of duplication has grown up over the years with firms in each country manufacturing exactly the same goods as their neighbours, but to differing technical standards (which were often designed with the precise intention of discouraging competing imports). The resulting over-capacity obviously cannot be sustained within the new single market. For example, four manufacturers supply the entire American market with domestic appliances, whilst the similarly sized EC market has 300 manufacturers of domestic appliances.

According to Amin Rajan in his book, *1992: A Zero Sum Game*, 'About half of the community's factories may close by the year 2000 before its industry is strong enough to reverse the American and Japanese onslaught. In the meantime, gains arising from this process will be modest. More likely they will be in the form of a zero sum game: winners will win only because losers lose, as in poker.'

WHAT DOES THE SINGLE MARKET MEAN?

Abolition of frontier controls Getting rid of customs barriers is designed to encourage trade and tourism and reduce administration costs. Computer-read Euro passports for everyone will also cut down on delays. However, fears have arisen over how to control the movement of drugs and of terrorists and criminals, though it could be argued that these are no longer purely national problems and should, in any case, be dealt with on a community-wide basis.

Removal of protectionist policies towards trade Getting rid of barriers to free trade such as tariffs and quotas against imported goods from the other EC countries has created the largest industrial market in the world. External trade with countries outside the EC will be based on the principle of 'reciprocity', which essentially means that 'if you grant us access to your markets, we will grant you access to ours'. Critics of the single market argue that the internal barriers will merely give way to external barriers against the rest of the world.

Many foreign companies have set up subsidiaries within the member states over the last few years. To guard against unfair trading practices, the EC has strengthened its laws dealing with the cut price 'dumping' of goods. (This is where goods are sold at or even below the amount that they cost to produce in order to undercut competitors' prices and force them out of the market.) The laws are aimed at companies that seek to evade import restrictions by operating 'screwdriver' assembly plants within the EC.

Common standards for goods The removal of differing technical standards and health and safety standards, which often served to protect home-produced goods against foreign imports has opened up the market and encouraged free competition.

Mutual recognition of qualifications This gives professionals such as accountants, solicitors and teachers the right to work anywhere within the EC.

Removal of restrictions on the movement of capital It is now possible to open a bank account or take out a mortgage anywhere in the EC. Use of the European Currency Unit (ECU) is to be expanded.

Common VAT rates Differing VAT rates in member states will be standardised. The introduction of VAT on all goods is likely to cause problems in Britain where, at present, essential items like food and clothes are not subject to VAT. Low income groups will be hardest hit.

Public authority contracts open to all firms Public authorities have to give firms from all member states an equal opportunity to tender for large contracts.

Common standards for television and satellite broadcasting This prevents member nations having incompatible systems. The 200 or so new TV stations will be subject to regulations which are designed to ensure that we will not be fed a diet of soaps, game shows and cop movies. However, sceptics have voiced doubts as to how many 'quality' programmes can actually be produced when so many stations exist. In a move designed to protect the European film industry from the influx of American feature films, stations will be required to reserve 60 per cent of air time for European made feature films.

Removal of state aid Governments are prevented from giving state aid to prop up their ailing industries, on the grounds that these constitute an illegal subsidy which distorts free competition.

Increase in regional aid This is intended to prevent a 'two-speed Europe' from developing as the gap that already exists between the richer Northern countries and the poorer Southern countries widens still further. The Commission is keenly aware that encouraging free movement could worsen regional imbalances as people and jobs will inevitably be drawn to the wealthiest regions. To combat this, the structural fund has been doubled, with most regional aid to go to Greece, Spain, Portugal and Southern Italy as well as Northern Ireland.

The common thread running through each of these measures is the clear determination to ensure that the rules of the game are the same for all – that any trading practices which could give particular firms an unfair advantage are removed. In the long run the creation of a single market which allows European firms to compete on equal terms must be a welcome development. However, it remains to be seen whether on balance British firms will gain from the increased opportunities open to them or whether they will be swamped by the competition coming in.

In the final analysis, Britain can only benefit from the single market if she can compete on equal terms. What is certain is that the removal of other barriers will count for nothing if the language barrier remains intact. Many more people in Britain will need to familiarise themselves with other European languages, particularly French and German.

The single market is here to stay. Estate agents have already begun advertising houses for 'Eurocommuters' near the air and sea ports with fast continental links. However, much still needs to be done over the next few years. There are plans for a European Central Bank, a Social Charter of workers' rights and, in time, full monetary union as well as some form of military integration. And it may not end there. Recent events have raised the question of whether we might one day form part of an even larger united Europe which includes the countries of Eastern Europe.

FINAL ACTIVITY

Pace Designs: designing a promotional campaign for a new product

BRIEF

You work for the advertising agency of Marston, Davis and Longton, who have just been approached by Pace Designs to produce a new promotion campaign for the national launch of their exciting new range of unisex jeans aimed at the 16- to 24-year-old target group.

1 Decide on a new name for the jeans and an appropriate slogan to be used in all the promotions. These must be in keeping with the image of the product and its market positioning.
2 Two commercials will be produced by your agency, to be shown on TV and in the cinema, which will cost £300,000 each to make. Suggest an outline idea or theme on which the adverts could be based.
3 Decide how you will allocate your promotion budget of £1.5 million between TV and press in order to reach the target group most effectively. Use Tables 2.2 and 2.3, which show advertising rates and circulation figures. Decide if any other sales promotions are to be used.
4 Design a full-page advertising spread for a newspaper or magazine, based on the theme you have chosen and incorporating all the necessary details.

Table 2.2 *Advertising rates for selected TV regions*

ITV Region	Maximum cost of a 30 second spot at weekday peak times (£)	Audience (number of ITV households '000)
Carlton/LWT (London)	74,000	4,565
Central TV (Midlands)	35,000	3,668
Granada TV (North West)	21,000	2,590
Yorkshire TV (Yorkshire)	15,000	2,301
Meridian (South and South East)	28,000	2,134
HTV (Wales and West)	15,000	1,842
Anglia TV (East)	20,000	1,665
Scottish TV (Central Scotland)	11,000	1,400
Tyne Tees TV (North East)	5,000	1,184
West Country TV (South West)	6,000	660
Ulster TV (Ulster)	3,000	491
Grampian TV (North Scotland)	2,000	479
Border TV (Border)	1,200	271

Source: *British Rate and Data (BRAD), June 1994; BARB Establishment Survey Report Q4 1993*

Table 2.3 *Advertising rates for selected newspapers and magazines*

Newspaper or magazine	Cost of a full page spread at standard rate (£)	Circulation (Average number of sales per month)
Daily Express	31,500	1,491,077
Daily Mail	32,760	1,758,994
Daily Mirror	32,800	2,695,266
Today	8,806	532,509
Sun	34,500	3,521,855
Daily Telegraph	43,500	1,033,573
News of the World	40,000	4,664,092
Radio Times	17,950	1,485,759
TV Times	14,400	1,021,966
Cosmopolitan	10,920	456,703
Mizz	7,750	183,960
Just Seventeen	7,930	226,562
Options	9,800	163,455

Source: *British Rate and Data (BRAD)*, June, 1994

Design and Development

IN ASSOCIATION WITH **SONY**

Introduction: what does design involve?

In the face of mounting evidence that buying decisions are rarely made on price alone, it is becoming increasingly obvious that good design is a powerful competitive weapon for business. Good design can also add value to a product, enabling it to be sold for more. Enlightened firms are already realising that good design can be one of the most powerful forces in creating distinctiveness, not just in terms of the features or look of the product, but also in terms of its quality and performance.

Good industrial design can influence not just what a product looks like, but how easily and cheaply it is made, how efficiently and reliably it functions and how well it can be displayed at the point of sale. Product design is therefore not only about **form** and **aesthetics** – that is, shape and appearance – but also about **function** – that is performance. However, industrial designers can only contribute fully if they are given a pivotal role in the development team rather than just being brought in as stylists at the end. They should be fully involved in every stage of the development process right through to advising on tooling and production systems.

Ideally, designers should work towards meeting a **design brief** or specification that describes the criteria or standards which the product design should achieve; though inevitably, any product design always represents a compromise solution between all the factors which have had to be reconciled. It is also influenced by a variety of constraints which place limitations on the designer.

Paul Kotler argues, in a recent article, *'Design' A powerful strategic tool*, that in order to succeed a company must 'seek to creatively blend the major elements of the **design mix**, namely performance, quality, durability, appearance and cost'.

Design influences the look of every product we see around us. This chair was designed by T. Dixon. Courtesy V & A Picture Library.

ACTIVITY

Analysing the factors involved in designing a new product

Look at the factors below, which might be taken into account by a design team working on a new product. State which element of the design mix is being considered in each case.

- How will inspection and testing for faults be carried out?
- Is the styling in keeping with the image of the product?
- Does the product have the latest technical functions the market wants?
- Can the design be simplified to make production easier?
- Are the properties of the materials and components suitable for the product's expected life?
- Can fewer moving parts be used?
- Is the product comfortable/practical to use?
- Can this design be made with the existing production facilities?
- Will the investment in the product be recovered over its life cycle?
- How good are the materials and components from suppliers?
- What are the distinguishing features of the product's exterior?
- How regularly will the product need maintenance/servicing?
- What operating/storage conditions will the product have to stand up to?
- Are the materials and components in line with the retail price?
- What safety standards and regulations will the product have to comply with?
- Can maintenance be carried out easily?

CASE STUDY

Ross – the English designer radio

British electronics firm Ross Consumer Electronics plc were doing even better than selling fridges to Eskimos – they were selling radios to the Japanese at the rate of 10,000 a year. The style-conscious Japanese loved the Ross Radio's uncluttered 'English' styling – a far cry from the usual high-tech Far Eastern look, with all its technological wizardry, that they are used to.

Ross Marks founded the company when he was 18, in his first term of a business degree course at the City of London Polytechnic. Having heard a lecture on how businesses are set up, he decided to go along to Companies House, which was only down the road. 'I had a pound in my pocket, so I decided to go down and register the name. The next thing was to ask myself what I was going to do with the company.' The answer was blank audio cassette tapes. This was still 1971 and they were not as yet widely available, so he decided to sell them by mail order. 'With mail order you get the money before you have to pay for the goods, so it's a way of starting up without having to get finance organised first.'

Since these early days, the company has come a long way, growing from being an importer of Far Eastern products to a manufacturer of audio electronics accessories, selling to 27 countries and with a current turnover of £6 million. The radio was, in fact, the second product which had tempted the Japanese to buy British. The company's earlier success was with a set of headphones designed by Graham Thomson of Brand New Limited, the product development wing of Michael Peters Limited, which gave Ross a more than 50 per cent share of the UK headphone market.

Once the decision to manufacture rather than import had been taken, efforts were concentrated on making the operation **capital intensive**, with large amounts spent on tooling, so that little labour was needed. The headphones were designed to be made using injection-moulding techniques so that a workforce of 10 could clip together 1,500 pieces in a working day.

It was the success of this venture that prompted the company to look into designing a radio and to use the same industrial designer again. There were no other portable radios around at the time that Ross Marks liked the look of. 'They were all black and chrome with ugly controls.' His plans for investing in the first radio to be designed and manufactured in Britain for 20 years won backing from the Design Council Consultancy Scheme, supported by the Department of Trade and Industry, which contributed 8 per cent of the £60,000 needed for tooling and design.

Having had the marketing flair to spot a gap in the market that he could fill, the next step for Ross was to approach Brand New again. The **design brief** was to create a radio that did not look like a Far Eastern product, would suit any room in the house, would appeal to all age groups and could be manufactured to retail at a price appropriate to the mass market target group. 'We weren't told what materials to use or how it should look. That was up to us', said Graham Thomson, who has since set up in business with his own design consultancy, Product First.

The eventual choice of design, from about 30 **concepts** Brand New presented, was influenced by the market research, which showed that most people tend to leave their radios tuned to a favourite station. Why bother, then, to have constant access to the controls? The design chosen by Ross was one which concealed all the controls apart from the on/off switch behind a hinged flap-open cover, making for a sleek, clean-cut design.

A moulded handclasp at the rear made an expensive carrying handle redundant. As well as the appearance, Thomson also worked on the layout of the internal components and advised on the selection of materials and on the tooling required for easy, low-cost assembly, with injection-moulding tools eliminating the need for soldering and screws. Working samples were then made up and tested. 'Alterations in tooling are expensive', says Marks. 'You can see potential assembly problems far more easily with a product in front of you.' Consumer trials proved favourable, so the decision was taken to go ahead with full production. Lessons learnt from the Japanese influenced the decision to subcontract much of the assembly to other companies. (This works out much cheaper as there are no overheads. If demand rises more subcontractors can be used, but if it drops the originating company does not face the problem of overstaffing.)

Launched for Christmas 1985, the Designer Radio won instant acclaim with its imaginative and innovative design. The initial total production run of 20,000 radios had to be quickly extended to 100,000 units a year. However, the product has since come to the end of its life cycle. Good design ensured that it sold for a much longer period than most fashion products.

Clearly, investment in good design has paid off for Ross. They have now moved on to investigating other products, which will no doubt be equally innovative. As Ross Mark's emphasises, 'We operate in a business environment which is **market led** and constantly changing. If you can develop an empathy with the industrial designer, you can hammer out product designs that will really set you apart from the competition.'

ACTIVITY

Analysing the stages involved in introducing a new product

Decide on the most logical order for the sequence of events involved in introducing a new product. What factors could influence the best order?

- Full-scale production
- Working samples made up and tested
- Models or prototypes made up
- Design chosen from concepts presented
- Design brief for product prepared
- Patent applied for
- Consumer trials on target group carried out
- Original idea or concept
- Gap in market identified
- Own designers or outside consultants from design agency approached
- Raw materials organised
- Tooling made up for manufacture
- Market research on consumer needs carried out

Designing a corporate identity

Most companies are aware that they are making a clear statement about themselves by the nature of the *products* they make. In addition, they are continually conveying messages about themselves, whether they realise it or not, through the quality of their *communications*. This takes place not just through the conscious marketing effort, but also through all the letters, forms, brochures, annual reports and other literature sent out, and even by the way the phone is answered. Powerful messages are also generated by the general *environment* of the firm, the interior and exterior style and appearance of its buildings and their general state of repair and cleanliness.

All of these factors combine to give an impression of the company's overall style and image as being reliable, well established, trendy, exclusive and so on. It is this broad spectrum of products, communications and general environment which makes up the **corporate identity**. If it is not coordinated through a concerted design effort across all three areas, a company may well find itself presenting a totally misleading image in the market place. In reality, firms cannot choose whether or not to develop a corporate identity. The only choice is between whether the identity is a well-designed, co-ordinated effect or an unconscious message haphazardly conveyed.

Michael Peters Limited have done some interesting work on creating corporate identities. When a client approaches them, they first gather data on the market, including details of the target groups at which the company's products and services are aimed. The **desired personality** which the company hopes to project is established. Its **positioning** in the market, in terms of how it stands out from the competition, is also assessed. A distinctive visual identity is then designed to reflect this positioning. In order to ensure that the company is conveying a consistent message and style, the new identity is communicated throughout product design and packaging, corporate and brand literature as well as buildings and vehicles. Designers at the group have developed corporate identities for organisations as diverse as the Alliance and Leicester Building Society, Safeways, PowerGen, the BBC and Corgi Toys, to name but a few.

Based on the 'no overtaking' traffic sign and brought to life by the oncoming car racing out of the lettering, Corgi's new logo expresses youth, vitality and fun. It also makes a clear reference to the company's business, unlike the previous Corgi dog logo. The new symbol is used on packaging, literature, advertising and trade show displays. In the year of the relaunched range, Corgi recorded a 60 per cent increase in sales value.

When PowerGen was created in 1989 as the first step towards privatisation of the Central Electricity Generating Board in the UK, Michael Peters were appointed to create a corporate identity for the new company. The new visual identity symbolises the harnessing of energy by man for the benefit of others. It has helped to establish the company as different from the old government-controlled organisation and has been widely acknowledged as reflecting the caring culture and commercial approach that the new company intends to build.

ACTIVITY

Do organisations have a clear corporate identity?

Give two or three words or phrases which sum up your perception of the image of the following organisations:

Channel 4	Harrods
MacDonalds	Marks and Spencer
The Body Shop	Midland Bank
British Rail	Sony

Products must satisfy consumer needs

The first requirement of a successful new product is that it must be geared to satisfying consumer needs. However, this is more easily said than done. In affluent Western societies today, a vast range of products and services exists to serve consumer needs. Many innovative firms are therefore going one stage further by attempting to stimulate subconscious needs. This new focus is evident in the approach adopted by one company, (quoted by the DTI in their survey of innovative companies), who argue that, 'You must get into the mind of the customer even when the customer does not know their own mind!' The challenge now facing marketers is that these **latent needs** are awakened only when the new product is first introduced onto the market. After all, how many people thought they needed a personal stereo, compact disc player or microwave oven until these products actually became available?

In his book, *The Design Dimension*, Christopher Lorenz describes the approach adopted by Sony. When Sony unveiled their new portable black-and-white TV set with an 8-inch screen in the USA during the 1960s, it was an immediate success. Yet only weeks earlier, General Electric had completed a major piece of market research on the potential of small, portable TVs whose findings included conclusions like 'people do not place a high value on portability of the TV set'. Rather than asking consumers to predict their feelings towards an unfamiliar product, Sony had instead observed the growing number of sets sold and the increasing number of TV channels and realised that these two factors would create a demand for a second set in many homes. Lorenz went on to add that, 'In effect, the company had looked beyond consumers expressed needs to their underlying behaviour patterns and had led the market by stimulating a new want. It has since done precisely the same with the video cassette recorder, Walkman personal stereo and the Watchman flat-tube TV.'

Clearly, companies with a successful record of product innovation are those who consistently manage to introduce products which satisfy the existing or latent needs of a target market. This sounds a very straightforward recipe for success. The fact is there are many pitfalls for the unwary. For one thing, the findings of market research surveys often provide a poor indication of the true sales potential of highly innovative products. It is notoriously difficult to gauge consumer reaction to radically different products which are unlike anything else on the market, since consumers invariably dislike products they cannot visualise.

The experience of the Post-it notepads developed by 3M is typical, where the marketing people were ready to scrap the project at an early stage because the product had performed so badly in the initial research studies. In this instance, the use of trial samples proved to be the key factor in gaining consumer acceptance and the familiar yellow note-pads have since become one of 3M's most successful products – no mean feat in a company that manufactures over 60,000 products!

Some would argue that if companies always heeded market research findings they would never launch radically different products at all. Certainly the lesson appears to be that damning research findings in the case of innovative products should be treated with a degree of caution in order to avoid the danger of rejecting potential winners. Decisions made on the strength of market research recommendations should, in any case, always be taken in the light of managers experience and judgement. In the most innovative companies, their 'feel' for the market is legendary. For instance, the Sony Walkman was launched despite research that warned it would be a complete flop. In the event, Sony went on to reap the marketing coup of the decade.

However, these examples do not indicate that market research evidence should be ignored as a matter of course. In the majority of cases properly conducted research is a reliable predictor of market potential. In fact, the penalty for introducing products which have been developed without reference to consumer needs can be high. The Sinclair C5 is a classic example of a product which, although it was extremely innovative, failed within a very short time of being launched. This was largely because the market need for an electronic vehicle with a limited carrying capacity and performance was never properly established. A full-scale market research survey was out of the question because of the emphasis on secrecy. Instead, a small sample of 63 families was shown the vehicle and allowed to drive it around a large room. The C5 was launched on the basis of this limited research and of course the personal conviction of Sir Clive Sinclair. In October 1985 the *Financial Times* reported that the receiver put the debts of Sinclair's C5 concern at £7.75 million. Nevertheless, it is interesting to speculate whether the C5 might have succeeded if it had been promoted as a golf trolley or invalid wheelchair. In other words, could it have survived if it had been designed to meet a specific consumer need?

ACTIVITY

Needs catered for by different innovations

What are the needs and requirements catered for by the following innovations?

Car phones	Infra-red alarm detectors	Disposable kitchen towels
Low-calorie drinks	Video-cassette recorders	Frozen ready meals
Cash machines	Solid emulsion paints	High speed trains
Non-stick pans	Personal computers	Satellite dishes
	Personal stereos	Photocopiers

The role of technology

The pace of technological change is such that new products are quickly superseded as competitors scramble to bring out even more advanced versions. In the nature of things it is obviously inevitable that successful products are going to attract imitators. However, it is the scale of competition today that is unprecedented. As Richard Brooks points out in his book, *The New Marketing*, 'Five years after the launch of its personal computer, IBM was fighting a new battle – not with the Japanese as everyone originally expected, but with low-wage companies in Taiwan and South Korea. By 1986 IBM's PC had become a commodity product and was being copied by more than two hundred firms.'

Firms need, therefore, to introduce a constant stream of new products. Few can aim to be as prolific as Hewlett Packard, who manage to generate ideas for eight new products a week! Yet all the signs suggest that UK firms, particularly in terms of creative ability, have the potential to exceed this performance. A recent survey by the Japanese Ministry of International Trade and Industry, quoted in *Winning Ways* by James Pilditch, claims that of the significant innovations since the Second World War, 6 per cent were Japanese, 14 per cent were French, 22 per cent came from the USA and a staggering 55 per cent were from the UK.

State-of-the-art technology has certainly been the key factor determining the success of Renishaw Plc, a British manufacturer whose touch-trigger probe is capable of measuring machined steel to accuracies of millionths of a metre. The probe, which has a 70 per cent share of the world market for such tools, is used on products ranging from car engines to the US space shuttle, where the accurate fit of the heat-shielding tiles is vital to the survival of the shuttle as it passes through the earth's atmosphere.

The role of technology is essential in stimulating a high level of innovation, particularly amongst the motor vehicle, electronic, aerospace, pharmaceutical and consumer goods industries. New technological advances can determine:

- **The kinds of products and services that are offered**, e.g. fax machines, satellite TV, digital audio tapes, cash dispensing machines, antibiotics, etc.

- **The kinds of raw materials that are available**, e.g. man-made fibres, biodegradable plastics, ceramic parts for car engines, aseptic packaging for products like fruit juices which previously required refrigeration, etc.
- **The ways in which products are designed and manufactured**, e.g. techniques like CAD have dramatically reduced the time taken to design and engineer new products and the use of robots has revolutionised production lines in industries like car manufacturing.

Given the crucial role played by technology in innovation it is obviously vital that companies keep an open mind towards emerging technologies. In 1938, an amateur physicist living in New York called Chester Carlson developed a process which he called 'electro-photography'. Carlson approached more than 20 companies to try and get them to develop his product, including RCA, IBM and General Electric, but was turned down by every one. Eventually, a small company called Haloid agreed to develop his process commercially. Haloid, which later became Xerox, is now one of the largest corporations in the USA – a success due in no small measure to the fact that the company was the first to spot the huge potential of photocopiers.

Clearly, then, firms need to be flexible enough to respond to each wave of technological progress as it occurs. Ultimately, those who are unwilling or unable to adapt to the rapidly accelerating pace of change are likely to face an increasingly uncertain future – witness the fate of many of the Swiss watchmakers who were slow in adopting quartz digital technology. However, market conditions are complex and there are many reasons why even products that are technologically superior do not automatically succeed. In the case of the Apple Macintosh computer, what should have been a huge sales advantage (that is, that anyone, not just computer experts, could learn how to operate the computer in as little as 20 minutes) counted for very little in a market where the need for IBM compatibility was the major consideration.

The importance of innovation

In the fiercely competitive trading conditions of the 1990s, innovation has emerged as the main battleground, with success being determined by the ability of companies to bring a constant stream of ever-more sophisticated products to the market ahead of their competitors. The rules of the game have moved on. Innovation was once regarded as essential for growth; today it has become essential for survival.

Rising standards of living and the pace of technological change mean that companies need to constantly update their products and services in order to cater for the latest customer expectations. It is all too easy to get left behind when yesterday's radical new extras, such as VCRs with Nicam digital stereo, become today's taken-for-granted features. The motor car industry illustrates the scale of this competition. Japan's eight car manufacturers change their models on average every 4.6 years. This compares with an average figure of 8.1 years for the three major US car makers and 12.2 years for European manufacturers.

UK firms clearly face a formidable challenge. By definition, those who do not view innovation as a priority have effectively opted for stagnation and eventual decline. The role of management is critical in nurturing a culture that actively fosters change and innovation. 'Our job', according to one chairman of a highly innovative company, 'is to make our products obsolete before our competitors do.' Innovation is often confused with invention and assumed to be the sole province of the Research and Development (R & D) department. The popular image of boffins in white coats conjuring up new inventions is clearly outdated. The reality is that innovation does not have to be technology-led. People from a wide variety of departments within an organisation are capable of thinking up ideas for new products or modifications to existing products.

Something old, something new

The innovation process is not just about radical new inventions, although these do sometimes occur. The existence of well-known examples of innovations based on *revolutionary* technological changes, such as the invention of robots, fibre optics, lasers and silicon chips, has unfortunately tended to perpetuate the myth that most innovations stem from this kind of creative breakthrough. In fact, the reality behind most product introductions is far less dramatic.

Innovations tend to develop more as a result of an *evolutionary* process: once a product has been introduced onto the market, the information provided as feedback from users is incorporated into later modifications and improvements, through continuous redesigns. The product thus evolves gradually in stages, via a series of small incremental steps, rather than as a giant technical quantum leap forward. The so-called 'block-buster discoveries' are, by definition, few and far between. After all, radically different products such as the TV, computer or aeroplane cannot be invented very often!

Most 'new' designs have in fact evolved from this process of continuous redesign or **iteration**, which refines the product into a version that is cheaper, offers more sophisticated features and is better designed in some way. Innovation therefore involves modifying old products as well as developing new ones.

Japanese firms, such as Sony, have consistently adopted a policy of re-innovation. In a recent speech, Sony's chairman Akio Morita summed up the company's attitude. 'The technology of one product spawns the more advanced technology for another. We would not have been able to develop the Trinitron TV, or compact disc and digital recording, if we had not known how to design and manufacture the generation of products preceding them.' He went on to add that creativity in **product planning** was also important. 'There was no new technology involved in the Sony Walkman. What we did was see the technology we already had in a totally new configuration.'

In this context, it is obviously essential for firms to develop products which are capable of being redesigned. Gardiner and Rothwell, in their report on Innovation for the Design Council, distinguish between **lean** and **robust** designs. Robust designs can be stretched to produce a variety of versions for different requirements which form a **product design family**. The Boeing 707 and Ford Cortina are both examples of designs which gradually evolved into a family of models, each new stage incorporating the latest technological developments. Robust designs like this have a greater degree of flexibility than lean designs which are not capable of being adapted when customers need change.

Should firms just stick, then, to redesigning and developing their tried and tested products? Clearly, this offers less financial risk in the short-term, but without a flow of new products a company is likely to stagnate and decline. Companies need, obviously, to get the balance right between revamping old products and introducing new ones. Manufacturers of coated products, 3M, who have a formidable reputation for innovation, demonstrate what can be achieved. With about 60,000 individual products ranging from Scotch tape to Post-it notes, they consistently achieve their target of deriving 27 per cent of their sales revenue each year from products or services that are less than five years old.

CASE STUDY

Sony – leading the field through innovation

Within the high-tech world of consumer electronics, where new product development is seen as a routine fact of life, one company stands out as being the most consistently innovative. During the course of its 48 year history, Sony has surprised and delighted consumers with a succession of ingenious gadgets: pocket-sized transistor radios; video cassette recorders; hand-held camcorders and portable compact disc players – not to mention the ever-popular Walkman personal stereo. Now as much a part of every young person's wardrobe as a T-shirt, pair of jeans and trainers, the Walkman took off to become the greatest marketing coup of the 1980s. What's more, like many earlier Sony successes, the Walkman managed to carve out for itself a whole new sector of the market – a market which it still dominates – despite the rash of 'copycat' products that inevitably followed.

A major factor underpinning the formidable Sony record on innovation has undoubtedly been the clear priority accorded to new product development. It is an emphasis that emanates from the top. As chairman and co-founder Akio Morita points out, 'We need to make our products obsolete before our competitors do.' To this end, the company employs some 9,000 engineers and scientists who rank among the most prolific in the world – creating between them an average of 1,000 new product designs each year!

Around 80 per cent of these designs are improved versions of earlier products, where existing technology is adapted to provide the latest features, better performance and often a greater degree of miniaturisation. The other 20 per cent are aimed at stimulating entirely new markets. So what factors explain this exceptional level of creative output?

Unusually for a high-tech company, Sony believes in fostering creativity by encouraging engineers to try their hand at technologies they have not formally studied. Engineers are, in fact, given the freedom to work on any project within the company which interests them. In addition, many would argue that the successes reflect Morita's view that an innovative company should not be afraid of developing the occasional product that turns out to be a dud. 'Don't worry,' he jokingly told the engineer given a ¥20 million budget to design the Walkman, 'if it fails, we can always take it out of your salary.'

Sony Corporation is also unusual in that it is one of the few truly international companies. Today, 65 per cent of the staff work outside Japan. Technology centres have been established in Europe, Australia and the US, as well as Japan. The latest Technology Centre at Pencoed in South Wales, which was officially opened by Her Majesty The Queen in October 1993, is destined to be the flagship of Sony's colour TV production in Europe. Sony has been successfully manufacturing colour TVs at its site in Bridgend for 20 years. The decision to transfer production of colour TVs to Pencoed was prompted by the need to expand output from the current level of one million sets per year to around 1.5 million. As ever, the company has defied market trends and despite the 12 per cent downturn in UK retail sales within recent years, sales of Sony TV sets have reached a record high. The new £147 million development at Pencoed and Bridgend with its state-of-the-art manufacturing facilities is designed to cater for the growing market demand and will be finally completed by 1995.

The popularity of Sony colour TVs is due, in no small measure, to the Quality Assurance methods which have helped to create their reputation for quality and reliability. Each new model undergoes the most rigorous endurance tests before it is launched. Sample sets are switched on, placed in a freezer for 48 hours at −10°C then baked in an oven at 50°C. Some are deliberately dropped onto a concrete floor to test rigidity and stability. Others are switched on for continuous periods equivalent to 15 years of normal use. Random sample checks are made on each day of production and if just one component in a set does not perform to Sony Standards then the whole batch is checked and, if necessary, rejected. As a result, the defect rate is now a minimal 0.5 per cent of production.

Part of the explanation for the continuing sales success is of course the company's legendary commitment to innovation, which results in some 30–40 new models being designed each year. The fact that Sony was first to the market with major new developments like Teletext and Fastext also provided the company with an important early sales advantage.

John Redwood MP opening the new Frame Manufacturing Operation at Bridgend

The pace of technological change today is such that only the most creative and innovative companies can expect to survive, let alone prosper, in the increasingly competitive market place of the future. However, all the evidence suggests that the researchers at Sony are capable of ensuring that the company continues to lead the field into the next century.

The need for teamwork

The lone inventor concept and the 'Eureka!' syndrome of product innovation are no longer applicable today, particularly as industrial engineering becomes more complex. Great design engineers like Robert Stephenson, the locomotive builder, and Isambard Kingdom Brunel, the civil engineer, possessed formidable abilities. However, with the information explosion that has occurred since their time, it is debatable whether one person is capable any longer of mastering all the specialist knowledge found in a variety of disciplines.

Teamwork is the approach adopted in today's enlightened companies who are committed to design, as being the best way to refine, develop and implement a complicated project. How should such multi-disciplinary teams be organised? As David Bernstein, who runs a successful design agency, points out, in a talk given at the London Business School, 'When a project is begun in one department and handed over to another, then inevitably some of the impetus is lost and much of the continuity and sense of ownership. The answer is frequently to create a matrix structure, a horizontal band across the vertical divisions, a project group, for example, cutting across the department divisions and consisting of members from each department.' The aim now is to change the traditional **linear** or sequential approach, where the research, design, production and marketing departments are brought in one after the other as the project progresses, to a **matrix** or teamwork approach whereby people drawn from different departments work together simultaneously on developing a project. The comparison is between running a relay race or playing in a football team.

Teamwork is vital in helping firms to maintain their competitive position. When Fuji first launched its throw-away camera, Kodak responded to the lucrative market sector which had been opened up by introducing its own disposable camera. A teamwork approach enabled Kodak to design and develop their new 'Fling' camera in record time. The company's computer-aided design system was *networked* so that all the people involved, including an outside firm of toolmakers, could work together simultaneously on the project.

Large companies organised on a **pyramidal** structure can often stifle innovation in their efforts to minimise risk. However, as James Pilditch points out in his book *Winning Ways*, innovative companies go to great lengths to cut through this hierarchy. At Texas Instruments they run an IDEA programme (Identify, Define, Expose, Act). Any young engineer could get $20,000 to test a new idea simply by convincing any one member of a large group of authorised technical staff that it was worth following. *Speak'n'Spell*, the voice synthesising device, was developed in this way. He went on to add that 'The essential point is to create teams that cut across all the usual departmental walls, then to free them from the normal procedures of the company's main business.' These teams in companies such as 3M and Hewlett Packard are like small entrepreneurial start-ups which are put together to come up with new products in any way they want. They let many ideas develop, then test them quickly on the market. Basically, they are a way of getting small company vitality into an established corporation.

The dangers of poor coordination

The use of teams of people brought together from different departments to develop a new product has proved highly effective at Baker Perkins (Now APV Baker), a heavy engineering company manufacturing machinery for baking and biscuit making. A development team might consist of members from different areas of engineering and from the sales, finance, marketing, manufacturing and industrial design departments. Such cooperation improves communication, avoiding the dangers of various departments pulling in different directions. These dangers are amusingly illustrated by Michael Smith, who runs Baker Perkins, in a series of diagrams on 'How not to design a swing', or 'The perils of poor coordination', quoted in Christopher Lorenz's book *The Design Dimension*.

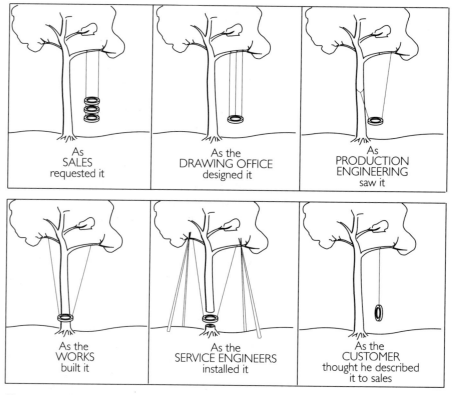

How not to design a swing

Marconi – meeting innovation face to face

Afavourite sci-fi icon, the home videophone has been 'just around the corner' for 50 years or more. However, it was not until April 1990 that the first prototype product was developed by GEC Marconi after 10 years of painstaking research and development. Nick-named ET by the design engineers because of the way the display and camera were set on a long neck, this early prototype was an exciting innovation. The idea is simple – a miniature camera transmits the caller's picture down a telephone line which is then displayed on a tiny television screen at the other end, but the technology required took almost seven years to develop and perfect.

The home videophone designed by GEC Marconi

As might be expected, the home videophone was the result of a major advance in research and development. Surprisingly, though, the breakthrough needed was in mathematics as well as electronics. Still pictures can be sent by fax machines – the images are converted into a digital code which is then transmitted along the telephone lines via a modem. However, this method could not be used for live images of people (which are moving rather than still) because the complex codes involved cannot be sent quickly enough down the telephone line.

Marconi's solution to the problem was to further refine the techniques of audio and video compression. A moving image is made up of a rapid series of still frames, each of which is only fractionally different from the previous one. The video compression technique enables moving pictures to be sent via telephone lines as only the codes for the parts of the picture that have changed from frame to frame are transmitted.

The development of a complex product such as the home videophone is a good example of the importance of teamwork. The project team at Marconi was made up of engineers drawn from a variety of areas: electronic design, mechanical design, production, marketing and so on. Close cooperation between different members of the project team meant that the design and development process was geared to the requirements of production from the outset. For example, the mechanical and electronic design engineers worked together to ensure that components such as circuit boards did not interfere with mechanical parts such as clips. Similarly, the production engineers' involvement ensured that the eventual design was capable of being assembled easily by unskilled operators.

To keep everyone informed of what was going on, a central database was set up which team members could access via their own workstations. As a result, engineers could approve, modify or reject proposed design changes at every stage of the development process. This attention to detail has paid off handsomely in creating a successful product that has achieved a high degree of market acceptance within a short time of being launched.

The need to shorten lead times

Olivetti used to take two years to introduce a new typewriter; now they can start to produce new designs in about two months. When IBM first introduced personal computers, they cut their normal development time from 24 months to 14 months forcing other competitors to try and follow suit. Cutting development times does not mean introducing poor products. In *A Passion for Excellence*, American authors Tom Peters and Nancy Austin describe how Xerox created a new product in 28 days that has since earned them £3 billion.

Once the decision has been taken to launch a new product, it is vitally important that the development time or **lead time** between initial design and full production is reduced as much as possible. If companies take too long to introduce a product, competitors will enter the market with similar products and erode potential profits. A study has shown that in consumer electronics, distributing a product six months late can cut life-cycle profits by about a third. More and more businesses today are therefore trying to cut lead times, a common aim being to halve them.

Those leading companies who have succeeded in meeting this challenge have done so by cutting product introduction times to the bone, making use of **computer aided design (CAD)** techniques. These have revolutionised the time needed to design and develop a product.

Advanced CAD facilities used in the design of products at Renishaw Plc

There are many advantages of CAD:

- Designers can create a greater variety of products. All dimensions within the design can be varied radically or by the merest fraction, as the designer wishes. The designer can sketch a basic shape for a product, produce a wire-frame model and a three-dimensional shaded model and show how all the parts used for the product are assembled together.
- The time previously spent on making models and prototypes to test the feasibility of the design can be saved, because the performance characteristics of the computer design, such as resistance to stress, can be analysed to a high degree of probability.
- The design can be modified at this early stage in the light of any problems which emerge, thus preventing the need for expensive reworking later. There is therefore a greater likelihood of the product specification being *right first time* when manufacture begins.

CASE STUDY

Rover – driving ahead with a new engine

The development of a major design innovation can provide a company with the crucial competitive edge it needs to survive in today's marketplace. The new K-series engine developed by Rover is a case in point. In the early 1980s, Rover was struggling to maintain its market position within the increasingly cut-throat home market which had traditionally been its stronghold. In the event, the £200 million spent on developing the new engine design has earned the company a string of awards, including the prestigious Queens Award for Technological Achievement in 1992. Most importantly, it has provided Rover with a much-needed stake in the European car manufacturing industry.

Launched in 1990, the K-series engines are designed to cater for the increasing consumer demand for cars which are environmentally-friendly yet offer a significant advance in power and performance. Accordingly, the 'lean-burn' technology which was developed reduces exhaust wastes to a level which, when coupled with a closed loop catalytic converter, not only meets current legislation but satisfies all known future emission standards. Aluminium replaces cast-iron for a much lighter and more economical engine. To overcome the fact that aluminium is weaker than iron, in what is probably one of the most innovative features, the design incorporates 10 long bolts which pass right through the engine from top to bottom. The bolts compress the sections of the engine like a giant sandwich. Under compression aluminium is at its strongest, creating an engine structure that is capable of withstanding the huge stresses experienced at high engine speed.

The K-series design could not have been made in its present form with existing metal-casting techniques. Rover therefore developed a new **Low Pressure Sand (LPS) casting process** which precisely reproduced the thin-walled engine structures demanded by the design. Using computer design data, a type of robot called a cyclobot finely machines the cast-aluminium blocks. Another major advantage of the design is that it is capable of being expanded into a whole new generation or 'family' of engine models. **Computer Numerically-Controlled (CNC)** machines can be reprogrammed to provide different tooling for manufacture. Any aspect of the engine design can thus be modified over a period of time because the existing machinery can be more easily adapted each time a new engine is developed.

The development programme for the K-series engines involved 73,000 hours and two million miles of testing spread across 875 prototype engines at a total cost of £200 million. This is in fact a very competitive figure for a complex project of this nature. The cost of this project would have been much greater without the use of advanced CAD methods, which allowed the internal dynamics of the engine to be simulated with a high degree of accuracy. Modifications and improvements could therefore be made before incurring the expense of tooling machinery for manufacturing the prototype.

The models incorporating the new K-series engines have proved a good match for the best of the European and Japanese manufacturers who have until now dominated the market for small and medium-sized cars. The Longbridge plant where the engines are manufactured is currently working at full capacity in order to meet the high level of market demand. Clearly, the investment of £200 million in this innovative engine design has paid off handsomely. Rover can look forward to a continued increase in sales, confident that the K-series engine promises a secure future in the European car manufacturing industry into the next decade and beyond.

The need for long-term investment

The costs of developing innovative new products in high technology industries and of installing automation and robotics are so great that there is generally a long **payback period** before the investment can be expected to yield any returns. It follows from this that if UK firms wish to match the performance of aggressive overseas competitors, they may need to forgo short-term profits in order to make the long-term investments which are essential for survival.

A recent report on innovation for the Design Council, by Paul Gardiner and Roy Rothwell, pointed to 'the problem of British firms adopting an increasing "cash flow" view of development activity, focusing on short-term projects that yield quick results instead of taking the longer-term view and investing in innovation'. They went on to add that British firms are often at a disadvantage compared to German and Japanese firms, because of the lack of City investors who are willing to take a long-term view and lend 'patient money'. In other words, City investors generally expect a quick return and are less prepared to make investments which take years to yield any profits – the so-called 'Jam today' mentality.

Private companies generally find it easier to adopt a committed policy of reinvestment than public companies, which have to explain to shareholders that their dividends are going to be lower for a few years because of money invested in developing new products. Tax policies in the UK are not very helpful either. Whereas companies can 'write off' spending on research, investment in product design and development is not allowable against tax.

The Staffordshire-based firm of JC Bamford Excavators, which manufactures earth-moving equipment, reinvests more than £20 million a year. Clearly, JCB's priorities of building up a sound operational base, rather than being concerned with short-term profits, are a lesson to other firms.

Testing in extreme climatic conditions at JCB

Many more UK firms will need to take a long-term view in order to keep up with the competition. This is especially important if firms are to invest in new technology such as computer-aided design and manufacturing or robotics, where the pay-back period is likely to be five years or longer. In view of this, firms who are concerned only with better and better figures over the next quarter or six months are likely to find themselves being gradually squeezed out by those who *have* invested in the future.

Taking the long-term view does of course mean accepting that though a new innovation can bring in vast profits it can also fail. As Gardiner and Rothwell emphasise, 'Innovation is inherently a high risk undertaking and one of the things we can be sure about is that there will be failures. Management must accept this and not use one failure as an excuse for withdrawing from the innovation race altogether.' It goes without saying that innovation is more likely to thrive in companies where people involved in projects that fail are not thought less of.

The importance of research and development

The pace of innovation in today's marketplace is such that it has become vital for firms to invest heavily in **research and development (R & D)** in order to maintain their competitive edge. Firms which do not accord R & D a central role in their operations have effectively made a decision not to be in business in 10 or 15 years' time. It is within the high technology 'sunrise' industries such as computers, automobiles, electronics, pharmaceuticals and aerospace that the costs of such investment are particularly large. By the same token, however, the potential rewards, if a new product does prove to be a winner, are also much greater.

Within the automobile industry, the R & D costs for a new car can amount to around £300 million. The bill for taking a new model from design to production can be as much as £700 million. With outlays like these, car manufacturers obviously have to produce in huge volumes in order to make a profit. According to one estimate, a minimum of five million vehicles needs to be produced simply to recover the investment in R & D. Phillips, the Dutch electronics group, argue that many electronics products today must capture an 8 per cent share of the world market simply to break even on R & D costs. Not surprisingly, even the largest companies find it difficult to produce in such volumes, which is why they tend to use components such as a particular engine across a number of models.

The time and level of investment required to introduce a new drug onto the market is also phenomenal. One study has estimated that on average it takes about 13 years and £85 million to take a drug from basic research to product launch. Some of this investment goes on the early 'weeding out' process. The pharmaceutical division of ICI considers approximately 10,000 new chemical compounds each year. Of these, probably no more than four will be taken into development. Only about one in ten eventually make it through the development process to reach the market. Even then, there is no guarantee of success. Inevitably, there are only a handful of drugs, which are capable of generating enough profit to offset not only their own development costs but also those of the failures, as well as the 'non-starters' which never get past the development stage.

However, the rewards can be great for those companies which are successful in producing world-beating products. The anti-ulcer drug, Zantac, produced by Glaxo, the UK's leading pharmaceutical company, is a prime example. It has become the world's top selling prescription medicine, generating £1.4 billion in revenues in 1989/90 and accounting at one stage for almost 50 per cent of the company's sales.

Within the aerospace industry, developing a new aero engine from drawing board to eventual delivery can cost as much as £2 billion. For this reason, aero engine manufacturers such as Rolls Royce are now seeking to improve and modify existing engines rather than incur the expense of designing completely new ones from scratch. For instance, their latest engine is said to have been developed at the relatively modest cost of £100 million. The development costs were reduced by taking the core of an existing engine, fitting it out with parts adapted from other units and then incorporating all the latest modifications. In addition, whereas in the past the company built as many as 39 test engines when developing a new aero engine, today eight or ten is enough as much of the early testing is done by computer simulation.

The importance according to R & D within Rolls Royce, where spending rose to a high of £253 million in 1993, has obviously been a crucial factor in explaining the company's expanding share of world markets. In the space of 10 years, Rolls Royce has increased its share from 5 per cent to the point where it now accounts for 20 per cent of civil engines made worldwide.

These examples taken from very different industries demonstrate clearly that despite the phenomenal costs, an increasing number of companies at the leading edge of technology view their commitment to research and development as an essential investment in the future.

FINAL ACTIVITY

Johnson Ceramics: designing a new product

GENERAL BACKGROUND

You work as a product designer for a design agency called First Editions and have just been consulted by a new client, Johnson Ceramics, who are based in Stoke-on-Trent, Staffordshire, and manufacture crockery. Martin Johnson, the firm's founder, has come to see you because he wants to extend the firm's product base by introducing a new range of coffee mugs. The company already has products catering for most needs, which retail through department stores, supermarkets and gift shops. However, Martin thinks there is a gap in the market for a really well-designed mug aimed at the 16–20 age group. The new coffee mug must be a good shape and size, practical to use and cheap to manufacture. It must also have a graphic design likely to appeal to this target group.

THE BRIEF

Bearing in mind the client's requirements you will need to prepare a presentation to the company, which will include a design drawing for your coffee mug, together with a written list of all the factors you took into account in planning the design which you are going to recommend to them.
The list below suggests some possible areas you will need to think about before you start designing.

1 List five questions which you would expect a short market research questionnaire to include.
2 What is the product specification for your mug?
    a) Shape Wide or narrow? Rounded or angular? Heat loss minimised? Easy to hold? Stability? Stand to protect surfaces? Stackable when stored?
    b) Size Capacity held? Weight when carried full? Size of handle?
    c) Materials Made from stoneware, bone china, special glass or plastic? Resistant to what temperatures? Resistant to staining? Porosity? Expected life? Easily breakable? Microwave/dishwasher safe? Suitable for everyday or occasional use? Cost?
d) Graphic design On one side or both? Colours or black and white? A few colours or a riot of them? Pastels or bold primaries? Distinctiveness? Theme — landscapes, birds, flowers, cartoons, people, geometrics? Can design be extended for a whole range? Overall style geared to target group?
3 Which factors do you think are going to be most important for your brief?
4 What production methods would you advise your client to use? Mass production or craft methods? Glazed or unglazed? Interior and exterior finish? Handle fixed on or moulded in one piece?
5 Why would you make up prototypes of your design?
6 How should samples be tested?
7 How much do you think your design of coffee mug should retail for?

Production

IN ASSOCIATION WITH

United Biscuits

Introduction: the role of production

By definition, manufacturing firms exist to manufacture or make a product. It is the value added by firms during the production process which enables them to sell their finished product at a much higher price than the pure cost of the raw materials used in their manufacture. For example, car tyres sell for far more than the rubber that they are made from, furniture for far more than the cost of the timber alone.

In order to increase the amount of value added, firms need to make the best possible decisions in three key areas of production: **scale**, **method**, and **location**.

In addition, they are continually striving to improve efficiency and thus increase their productivity levels, in order to survive in a climate of increasing overseas competition.

ARE FIRMS GETTING BIGGER?

There is a growing trend, both within individual industries and in terms of total manufacturing output within the UK, for production to be concentrated more and more into the hands of a few large firms. According to the report of the Royal Commission on the Distribution of Income and Wealth, the 100 largest manufacturing companies employ roughly one third of the labour force and account for approximately 35 per cent of total net output. In fact, the scale of operations of some firms today, and in particular of the multinationals, is so vast that their production processes are split between different countries.

Firms can grow in size by means of:

- **Organic growth** Firms expand by taking on more employees, investing in more machinery, buildings and so on.
- **Acquisitions or mergers** Firms expand by joining together to form a single, larger organisation.

The trend towards concentration of production into a smaller number of firms has been mainly due to the increase in the number of mergers. In recent years, most mergers have been **conglomerate mergers**, where firms in different industries have joined together, **diversifying** their product base. This avoids the risks inherent in limiting their operations to a narrow range of products in one industry – that is, the dangers of putting 'all their eggs in one basket'.

However, the diversification process can be taken too far if firms expand into many unrelated industries in which they have no expertise. The only answer may then be to sell some of their **fringe** activities and concentrate on those they define as **core** activities, a process which can prove very lucrative.

Overall, this trend towards larger firms can be attributed to the cost savings which result from an increase in the scale of production.

Scale of production

Large firms are able to produce their goods at a more competitive price than small firms because their fixed costs are spread over the larger number of units which are produced.

Once gained, this competitive edge becomes self-perpetuating, enabling large firms to expand their market share still further. Smaller firms that cannot afford the initial outlay which makes these savings possible, and therefore cannot operate as cost-effectively, are gradually squeezed out unless they can survive by producing for a specialised area of the market. Rolls Royce does this in the car market where the big three companies, Rover (35.9 per cent), Ford (29.5 per cent) and Vauxhall (16 per cent), account for over 81 per cent of cars produced.

As firms get bigger they gain the benefits, in a variety of areas, of being able to spread costs and make savings by operating more efficiently. These are known as **economies of scale**. Apart from the **internal** economies of scale (see Table 4.1) possible within the firm, there are also **external** economies which can result from firms grouping together, such as the presence of components suppliers nearby, the use of one firm's end product or even its waste as raw material for another firm, the sharing of **infrastructure** like transport facilities, public utilities, schools, hospitals etc.

Table 4.1 *Internal economies of scale*

Type of economy	Enables firm to:
Purchasing	Buy materials more cheaply taking advantage of bulk discounts.
	Employ trained buyers who can negotiate the best deals.
Production	Use mass-production techniques to speed up and increase production.
	Afford to buy large, specialised, technically advanced machinery.
	Use specialised division of labour.
	Transport materials in bulk, often using their own transport fleets.
Risk-bearing	Afford to take more risks with launching a new product, as with a diversified range of products they always have others to fall back on if one fails.
	Sustain financial losses to a certain degree.
	Afford to employ an R & D department.
Financial	Borrow more easily as they have greater reserves and are perceived as being more credit-worthy by lenders.
	Obtain loans at more favourable rates of interest.
	Use their retained profits or reserves to finance projects.
	Afford to use the services of accountants and other financial advisers.
Marketing	Afford to advertise extensively, as the additional cost per unit produced is small when spread over a large output.
	Afford to employ specialist sales staff and run advertising departments.
Administrative	Sustain high overheads spread over greater output.
	Afford the higher salary packages necessary to recruit the best managers.
	Afford to install sophisticated computerised systems for controlling and monitoring the business.

Of course, an increase in the scale of operations does not lead solely to benefits such as cost reductions and improvements in efficiency. It can also lead to **diseconomies of scale**, such as excessive **bureaucracy**. Stemming from the need to introduce proper methods for dealing with communication and record-keeping, these same administrative systems can stifle the company with red tape. Large, unwieldy firms often lose their capacity to innovate and become unable to respond to changes in the market.

To overcome these problems, the majority of large firms now split their organisations into smaller divisions, which function independently on a day-to-day basis yet remain within the overall control of the parent company. They therefore operate, in effect, as smaller firms.

Method of production

The decision as to which production method a firm should adopt is influenced by the nature and variety of the products, market factors like the size and frequency of orders and the stage of development reached by the firm.

At one end of the scale is the type known as **job production**, based on 'one-offs' or small orders, often of luxury goods. This can be carried out on a small scale, as with custom-made clothes, or on a large scale, as with shipbuilding and aircraft manufacture. This type of production is **labour intensive**, either because a skilled workforce is required due to the nature of the work, or because the volume of production is too low for any major investment in machinery to be justified. It is the method most often used by start-up businesses.

Once demand increases and the design of the product is capable of being simplified and replicated to a certain standard, then it becomes both economically worthwhile and technically feasible for **mass production** techniques to be employed. Mass production involves making large volumes of identical products to the same standard, at a low unit cost. Products can be mass produced in batches or as a continuous flow.

The second type, **batch production**, is a more efficient method than job production as the work process is divided into its component operations. Each operation is completed for the whole batch of items being produced before the next operation is carried out. Batch production accounts for 75 per cent to 85 per cent of total production in Western countries.

The third type, **flow production**, is the most efficient method of all. Once the work on one operation is completed, the items are passed as a continuous flow to the next stage without having to wait for a batch to be completed as in the previous method. This is a very **capital intensive** type of operation because an automated production line requires a heavy initial outlay.

Longer production runs are common in mass production, where the variable costs of producing each item are reduced as experience is gained in the production process. This acquiring of experience is called the **learning curve**. When high volumes of goods are produced, unit costs fall.

The degree of job **specialisation** involved in flow-production processes creates a highly defined **division of labour**. Henry Ford's idea of dividing up the task of making a car into many separate operations, each simple enough to be done by one person, enabled the number of cars produced to increase dramatically and caused production costs to fall. His methods meant that a Model T Ford previously made in 12.5 hours could be built and tested in 1.5 hours.

Table 4.2 *Characteristics of each method of production*

Characteristic	Job	Batch	Flow
Size of demand	Demand is small. Manufacture of a single complex product or small quantity. Selling aimed at particular customers or firms in specialised markets.	Demand increases. Manufacture of a product in stages. Each operation for a batch completed before the whole batch moves onto the next operation. Selling aimed at a wider market.	Demand is regular and long term. Manufacture of a simplified and standardised product in large volumes. Selling aimed at national or international markets.
Quantity of products	Single product or small quantity produced.	Batch or group of products produced, usually in small quantity, before next batch started.	Large quantities produced.
Variety of products	Very flexible system. Enables large variety of products to be manufactured, geared to customer specification.	Still fairly flexible. Products more standardised but can vary from batch to batch, so can still be geared to customers' needs.	Not flexible. A limited range of products manufactured. In large-scale operations a variety of production lines can be used to provide a wider range of products.
Type of workforce	Skilled workers needed with a high degree of technical expertise and the ability to adapt. Can be a large workforce if a technically complex project is involved.	Less skilled workers needed who are skilled in one operation rather than in a whole task. Skilled quality control and maintenance workers needed.	Unskilled workers used, who perform a limited operation which they repeat over and over again. Efficient planning and control system needed to manage production.
Worker satisfaction	Worker motivation enhanced. Each new job presents a different challenge, so they need to be adaptable. Workers gain satisfaction from being responsible for the complete product.	Less worker satisfaction as jobs are less skilled. Workers are not involved with product from start to finish.	Difficult for workers to get satisfaction from their jobs as they tend to perform mechanical, repetitive tasks, many of which have been automated in recent years. Workers are only involved in a small part of the job cycle.
Type of machinery used	Generally less technically complex machinery used. More emphasis on the technical expertise of the operator. Wide range of machines needed for different jobs.	Less machinery used than in job production, but more complex as emphasis is on capability of machines rather than on the skill of the workers. Machines need to be retooled for each batch.	Technically complex machinery needed to produce standardised products. High investment in machinery presumes steady market demand.
Layout of plant	By fixed position.	By process.	By product.
Costs of production	Variable production costs are high, particularly labour costs, but fixed costs are low.	Costs are lower than in job production. Planning needs to be efficient so that production runs are as large as possible to spread costs over many units.	Fixed costs are high initially to start up the production line but variable production costs per unit are lower than in other methods.
Problems	Expensive form of production. Difficult to organise if production is technically complex.	Workers and machines can stand idle if one operation for a batch takes longer than another.	The processes on a traditionally organised production line are interdependent, so if one section is disrupted by a strike or if a bottleneck occurs, the whole line has to stop.

CASE STUDY

*Ross Young's –
pizza production*

Centuries after its origination in Southern Italy, pizza has become one of Britain's most popular snack foods. Consumption has risen faster than any other type of frozen food so that from virtually nothing ten years ago we now eat almost £150 million worth of them a year. Ross Young's, the frozen food division of the United Biscuits Group, has a 50 per cent manufacturing share of this fast growing market.

United Biscuits is a leading international snackfoods group with a turnover of over £3.45 billion in 1994 and a workforce of 39,352 worldwide. It comprises four principal operating divisions – McVitie's Group, the UK's number one biscuit producer and a strong number two in Europe, with long-running favourites such as Digestives and Penguins; KP Foods Group, the number one savoury snack company in Europe with products such as Hula Hoops and Roysters, and a market leader in South East Asia; Ross Young's, manufacturer of frozen and chilled foods and the UK's leading producer of pizzas, desserts and seafood products; and Keebler Company, the USA's second largest producer of cookies and crackers, with a stake in the savoury snacks market.

Given the extensive range of household-name brands produced by the group, it is hardly surprising that United Biscuits have over the years earned themselves an enviable reputation for successful product innovation. The introduction of McVities Pizza Slices provides a prime example. Since their launch in 1987 when they were voted the top new frozen food product of the year, they have captured a sizeable chunk of the growing market for pizzas and today sell at the rate of £15 million a year.

The factory at Grimsby in Humberside which makes the Pizza Slices is now the largest pizza factory in Europe. The use of 'state of the art' production machinery enables the factory to produce up to six million pizzas per week, including 'own label' brands for leading retailers such as Marks & Spencer, Sainsbury and Tesco.

One of the major processing technologies used in the factory is the 'Sheet and Cut' process. The first stage in this highly mechanised operation is where flour, fat, yeast, seasonings and water are beaten together in giant mixers which can each process 1.5 tonnes of dough per hour. The dough is rolled into a sheet as it passes through rollers and is cut into slices by special rollers positioned above. Next, the slices are baked in 80 feet long ovens and afterwards cooled by being passed through a forced cooling unit. The slices are then passed under a series of machines which deposit the right amount of sauce, cheese and garnishes, such as ham and peppers, onto each base.

Once the pizza slices are assembled, they then pass through a spiral freezer, which conveys them on a reverse 'helter skelter' from the ground floor to the upper floor through an extremely cold environment, until the temperature of the pizzas is down to –18°C. Finally, the slices are shrink-wrapped and marked with a 'Best Before' expiry date before being packed in cartons and taken to the cold store.

At each stage of the process, the pizzas are checked to ensure that the individual weights of ingredients, the distribution of the toppings, as well as overall appearance and flavour are all correct. Samples are also taken for laboratory testing to ensure that no harmful bacteria and other micro-organisms are present.

The investment in this and other state-of-the-art production technology is likely to prove an excellent long-term investment for Ross Young's. In total, the new mechanised production lines, which are capable of making well over 50,000 pizzas per hour, are clearly designed to meet the ever-growing demand in the market for pizzas through the 1990s and beyond.

CASE STUDY

*Oxford Magnets –
body imaging
machines*

The special electromagnets made at Oxford Magnets are used in equipment which generates images of the body. These are of the same quality as X-ray images but without the risks associated with the small amounts of radiation in X-rays. Oxford Magnets' customers are just three companies, which use the magnets in their own equipment to make the complete the diagnostic units. These sell mainly to hospitals in the USA, which can pay the $1.5 million to $2.5 million needed for a complete unit.

The patient lies on a bed which slides into the diagnostic machine containing the large electromagnet. The magnetic signals sent out by different molecules in the body in response to a radio frequency pulse are sent to a computer, which processes the information and produces an image on the scan.

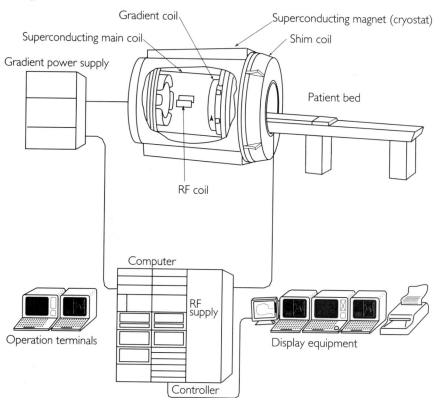

Diagnostic unit, showing body-imaging electomagnet

The company produces over 300 magnets a year, each one selling for approximately £240,000. Most of this price is accounted for by the cost of materials, particularly the special wire and the liquid helium used for cooling. Each packaging crate alone costs over £2,000! The special wire is expensive because it has the property of superconductivity – very high electric currents can be passed through it, yet virtually no heat is generated.

Each magnet is individually designed to the customer's specifications. All the raw materials are bought in and assembled in a three-stage process, each stage taking place in a different area of the factory.

Danger signs warning of the magnetic field alert visitors to the fact that the first area in the manufacturing process is being approached. Here, the electromagnetic wire is wound with great precision onto an aluminium drum which looks like a giant cotton reel. The need for accuracy is so great that computers are used to plan how the last 5 per cent of wire should be wound onto the drum. The second stage is where the coiled electromagnet is placed in a giant vacuum flask or cryostat. Lastly, the whole cryostat is cooled down by using liquid helium at –269°C. Final testing and quality control checks are exhaustive, taking about six weeks. The test results then have to be sent to the customers for their approval before shipment can be authorised.

The fact that each electromagnet is assembled from start to finish by a team of four skilled people, each responsible for a particular stage in the production process, ensures that workers have ultimate responsibility for quality control and are motivated by a sense of pride in the finished product.

Discussion point

Refer back to Table 4.2. How closely does the production process at Oxford Magnets match the general characteristics of job production?

CASE STUDY

British Steel – the Scunthorpe works

Scunthorpe is one of British Steel's four **integrated** steel plants and is capable of making more than four million tonnes of liquid steel each year. So how does Scunthorpe manage to produce steel at this rate?

Molten iron is produced by feeding a blend of coke (made from coal), iron ore and limestone into the top of the blast furnace, where a blast of hot air is blown through the bottom to fan the mixture to a white-hot intensity. The molten iron produced flows to the bottom, where it is tapped off on a regular basis. Raw materials are continuously poured into the top whilst iron is tapped off below.

Next, molten iron is loaded into a basic oxygen converter together with about 25 per cent scrap steel. A water-cooled lance is then lowered and oxygen blown through at more than twice the speed of sound.

Samples are then taken, and if the batch is ready the whole converter is tilted so that the steel can be run off into a ladle. While the steel is in the ladle any additions are made according to customer requirements. For example, tungsten can be added to provide sharp cutting edges for saws, knives and scissors.

In the past, most steel was poured from the ladles into ingot moulds, before being rolled. Nowadays, most steel is taken straight from the ladle while it is still molten, to be cast in water-cooled copper moulds. Continuous casting methods enable a number of ladles of the same grade of steel to be dealt with in one go, without needing to stop the machine to readjust it for each batch.

Steel from Scunthorpe has been used in everything from the construction of the Humber Bridge to staples, Brillo Pads and wire coat hangers. The plant has also supplied steel for the building of the Channel Tunnel and for the country's tallest building, 50 floors high, which has been built at Canary Wharf in London's Docklands.

Discussion points

1 Which parts of the process are examples of flow production?

2 Refer back to Table 4.2. How closely does the production of steel at Scunthorpe match the general characteristics of batch production?

Steel production at British Steel in Scunthorpe

CASE STUDY

Vauxhall Motors – production of the Astra

State-of-the-art production technology, computers and robots are all being used to build the Astra range at Vauxhall Motors, Ellesmere Port in Cheshire. General Motors, Vauxhall's US-based parent company, have invested over £400 million during the 1990s in new production facilities as a recognition of the plant's future potential.

In fact, Ellesmere Port was first chosen by General Motors for development in 1962. Government regional policy encouraged Vauxhall's expansion away from its Luton site in the then prosperous South East, as part of the drive to create employment in the declining manufacturing areas. The 4,200 jobs at the plant play a vital role in Cheshire's economy.

As with many products today, the Astra was designed with streamlined manufacture in mind. In fact, the computer design influenced every aspect of the production process from tooling of machines to plant layout and modular assembly. This largely explains why **automation** has been so successful. Unlike other plants which adopted wholesale automation with no restructuring beforehand, the automation here was applied to a completely reorganised and simplified production line. Robots are used extensively at the plant because they ensure a level of consistent quality that even the most skilled and dedicated employees cannot achieve week after week. They also handle heavy, demanding and repetitive tasks, which people generally dislike.

Ellesmere Port is an example of an **assembly line process**, where components, some of which are manufactured in-house and some of which are manufactured by other companies, are put together or assembled at the plant. Ultimately, about 3,900 components made up of 14,000 smaller components in all, will have come together in making an Astra car or van. The whole assembly process takes about 30 hours from beginning to end.

The starting point for the process is when steel sheets are fed into huge presses that stamp out panels for the Astra body, in a press shop which could take in three good-sized Wembley pitches.

The underbody, which forms the basis of the car, is joined together by robot welders and then transferred by an overhead rail to the computer-controlled body framing line, where the basic shell is formed. A conveyor belt called a 'skid' transports the underbody, which is marked by a 'Magna Code' similar to the magnetic bar codes used on goods in shops, so that the framing line robots can identify what type of body style is being handled.

In addition, computer control of the body framing line ensures that the right assemblies are delivered at the right time, all of which rules out any risk of a robot trying to weld an Astra's underbody to a van's sides! Once the body building process is underway, the plant's computer automatically reorders the components which have been used.

Doors, bonnet and wings are added and the 'body in white', as it is now known, then moves to the paint shop for anti-corrosion treatment, priming and then six layers of paint, as part of a ten-stage process, before moving to the trim shop.

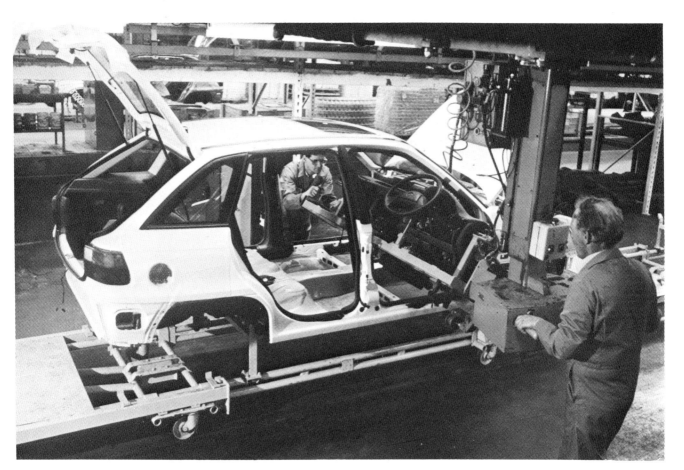

Car Production at Vauxhall Motors

Using the system of modular assembly, each pair of doors is first removed from the painted vehicle and taken away from the main assembly line for glass, fittings and trim to be added. This improves access to the car's interior once the doors are off, eliminates congestion near the assembly line and enables the cockpit (facia) to be inserted into the vehicle as an assembly.

At the final stage, seats, axles, petrol tank and engine are fitted, the wheels are bolted on and doors are refitted. The finished car then goes through stringent quality control checking stations, including being passed through bright, flaw revealing lights and being driven on rollers which simulate road conditions, in order to monitor on-road performance.

It is a tribute to the unique skills which only people can contribute that the process, which uses the latest in automated manufacturing techniques, ends with a sample of each day's production being scrutinised by eagle-eyed inspectors against a checklist of 200 points to ensure the highest level of quality control.

Location of production

What kinds of factors do firms consider when deciding where to locate? The eventual choice is usually based on a combination of factors, though sometimes one will exert a dominant influence. Industrialists will consider the presence of raw materials, power, markets, transport and labour, physical site characteristics and the availability of planning permission and government grants.

However, it is becoming recognised that decisions are not always made on such rational economic grounds and that irrational motivating factors also play a part. The concept of **rational economic man** is being questioned, with the realisation that human decision makers are influenced by their prejudices and perceptions of an area. Increasingly, it is also being realised that decision makers tend to behave as **satisficers**, being satisfied with a compromise location, rather than as **optimisers**, going all-out to find the elusive 'right' or optimum location. In other words, most decision makers are not prepared to search indefinitely for the perfect location. They tend, in any case, to make a decision based on the limited amount of information they have researched.

RAW MATERIALS

These can be minerals like iron or coal or, more commonly today, components, which may be the semiprocessed or finished products of other firms. Nearness to raw materials was by far the most influential factor in the early days of the Industrial Revolution, when transport facilities were poor.

A raw materials orientation is *still* important today if the materials:

- **Lose weight in processing**, as in the sugar refining industry. Raw sugar is one eighth of the weight of sugar beet, which is why the factories are located in the growing areas like East Anglia.
- **Are perishable**, as in the fruit canning industry. Fruits, especially soft fruits, go bad quickly and are easily bruised when transported.
- **Are of low unit value**, as in the copper smelting industry. Smelting is done in the mining areas because the ores contain only about 7 per cent copper and the rest is waste rock. This makes transport of copper ores uneconomic.

The pull of heavy raw materials has declined as better technology has reduced the amounts needed. For example, the production of pig iron now takes less than one ninth the amount of coal needed in 1750. In fact, most modern steelworks are no longer near deposits of iron and coal as they used to be, but tend now to be located on the coast, as they rely on cheap iron ore imported from abroad.

POWER

During the Industrial Revolution, factories using coal as a **primary fuel** developed on the coalfields. This pattern of industrial areas located on coalfields is still evident in Britain today, as a historical relic of our early industrialisation. However, the use of electricity, as a **secondary fuel** distributed everywhere through the National Grid, has made possible greater dispersion. Today's industries are **footloose** – freed from a power orientation; though some industries which are hungry users of power, like aluminium smelting, are still tied to sources of cheap electricity, and so tend to be located near hydro-electric plants.

MARKETS

As the pull of raw materials and power sources has declined, nearness to markets has become the most important factor, especially for industries like drinks manufacturers where the end product is **weight gaining**. It is not worth transporting what amounts to flavoured water long distances, when the water can be just as easily added near the markets. Market orientation is also important in industries where the end product is **perishable**, like bread, or where it is **cheap and bulky**, like bricks, so is not worth transporting far. It is not just the size of the market which is influential, but also the purchasing power of the people. As most goods are now being produced for national or even international markets, a location near good transport links that makes **access** to major markets possible is becoming increasingly important today.

TRANSPORT

Transport costs are complex. Costs do not rise proportionately with distance. Short hauls are, in fact, more expensive per kilometre as the handling, clerical and insurance costs still have to be paid even if the journey is short. Nor is weight the only influence on transport costs. For example, cotton bales are expensive to transport even though they are light, because they are so bulky. Generally bulk goods are best transported by rail over long distances.

The best location for footloose industries is tending to become the most **accessible** site, where components can be easily assembled and finished products distributed quickly. The importance of this trend can be seen by the rate at which factories are growing up along the motorways and main railways radiating out from urban areas.

LABOUR

This is not a very important locational factor, a trend which is likely to continue as machines replace jobs previously done by people. However, some industries are still labour intensive, such as clothing manufacture, where labour costs account for a high percentage of the costs of the finished product. Certain industries rely on a pool of highly skilled labour, such as jewellery making and clock manufacture.

PHYSICAL SITE CHARACTERISTICS

Large plants like car works, oil refineries and iron and steel works require vast amounts of flat, cheap land with a low amenity value, such as reclaimed marsh land. Nearness to water for cooling, washing or use in the actual process is often important. Over half of Scotland's whisky distilleries are sited around the Moray Firth, where the best water, which has drained through the peat, is found!

GOVERNMENT INTERVENTION

Since 1945, governments have intervened in location decisions to prevent the division of Britain into 'two nations', a prosperous core region in the South East surrounded by declining peripheral areas in Scotland, Wales and the North. The declining, coalfield-based heavy industries which were important in the early stages of the Industrial Revolution are found in these peripheral areas, whereas the newer growth or light industries which are footloose have tended to be attracted to the markets of the South East.

Successive governments have adopted regional policies in order to redistribute wealth and employment more evenly and halt migration to the South East, in an attempt to prevent the growing divide within Britain. Expansion in the prosperous core has been controlled by refusing planning permission, whilst at the same time relocation to the **assisted areas** has been encouraged by the offering of incentives, such as a 15 per cent grant towards capital expenditure on plant, machinery and buildings or works, plus £3,000 for each new full-time job created. A total of £6.7 billion has been paid by the government in grants since 1972. Though many firms have relocated, just how successful these measures have been in bringing about long-term changes in Britain's industrial pattern is debatable.

In January 1988, the government ended the regional development grant system. Regional **Selective Assistance** is now available for approved projects in the Assisted Areas, **Urban Programme areas** and **Coal Closure areas**. The companies must demonstrate a need for assistance for a project that is commercially viable and creates or safeguards employment. They will then be entitled to claim the minimum amount needed to ensure the project goes ahead. The DTI will also pay two thirds of the cost of consultancy projects in a variety of areas such as marketing, design, business planning, financial and information systems and quality control systems.

CHANCE FACTORS

William Morris, founder of one of Britain's earliest car firms, decided to locate a works at Cowley near Oxford, because he happened to notice his father's old school there up for sale. The Rover Group's car works now on this site employs 4,500 people. Could the works have succeeded equally well if he had chosen Aberdeen or Penzance? What *is* certain is that if the location had been a poor choice in terms of the factors discussed previously, it would not have survived for long.

How influential is the *perception* of an area held by decision makers, whether they be individuals or committees? Location decisions should not just be made on the basis of the managing director finding a good golf course nearby! Nevertheless, a growing awareness of the influence of image explains why the assisted areas now put as much effort into improving the amenities and the often blighted landscapes of their areas as they do into building factories and improving roads.

WHY DO INDUSTRIES TEND TO REMAIN IN THE SAME LOCATION?

Once an industry has become established in an area, it will often continue to survive even when the original advantages of its locating there have long disappeared. The textile industry in West Yorkshire grew up originally because of the availability of wool from Pennine sheep and because local coal could be used to power the machines. Neither of these factors applies any more, yet the industry still continues in the area.

This phenomenon of **industrial inertia** occurs mainly because the investment in fixed assets – buildings and machinery – is so great. This, coupled with the presence of a pool of skilled labour nearby, makes it very difficult to abandon the site and start afresh. In any case, completely new or **green-field** sites are difficult and expensive to set up because of the additional infrastructure needed, such as the roads and services which have to be provided.

ACTIVITY

*Selecting
locations of
industries*

Key Coalfield · Low grade iron ore · Marshland · Highland · Farmland · Deep water channel · Motorways · Main roads · Secondary roads · Railway lines · Power Station

Decide which of the sties marked A–H would be the best location for each of the industries listed below, giving at least two reasons to explain your choice in each case.

Shipbuilding
Car assembly
Oil refining
Sugar-beet refining

Jewellery manufacture
Aluminium smelting
Steel production
Electronic engineering

Hodder & Stoughton Educational © Permission to photocopy for classroom use only.

*Improving
efficiency: the
way forward*

What constitutes efficient production? Most firms would say that to reduce costs and improve quality would be a sure-fire way of beating rivals and ensuring commercial success. Important as they are, though, to get these factors right is still only part of the answer. Increasingly, in the current climate of over-capacity, worldwide competition and rapid technological change, firms must also be able to compete on factors other than price or quality. They must offer a much wider range of products, by being able to adapt their production process quickly in response to changing market demands and by reducing lead times – the time taken to develop a new product until it is ready for full production.

THE IMPACT OF AUTOMATION

The widespread automation of production processes which has been advocated in recent years is no longer seen as a universal solution for industry's problems.

There is no shortage of examples illustrating the benefits of automation. In addition, more advanced robots are continually being developed. For example, Ford has just developed the world's first 'seeing' robot. A magnet mounted on the robot's arm collects an engine part such as a crankshaft from storage. The robot identifies it by 'seeing' the part's shape and comparing it to information stored in a memory bank. The part is then placed with pinpoint accuracy on the production line.

Undisputed benefits such as these have unfortunately prompted business advisers in the last decade to advocate the wholesale adoption of automation. Many firms have been intimidated into spending vast sums of money on unnecessary technology by simplistic slogans such as 'automate or liquidate'.

Car Production at Vauxhall

However, unless the design and organisation of the production line are simplified and streamlined beforehand, automation will merely accentuate the existing problems, not solve them. Nothing less than the complete reorganisation of the whole production line will work, as the introduction of automation on its own merely speeds up an existing inefficient process and adds the purchase and upkeep of the machinery as an extra cost burden. When complete reorganisation does take place, though, extending from simplifying the original design of the product right through to changing the plant layout, as Vauxhall have done with their Astra production line, then the benefits can be substantial.

CASE STUDY

IBM – advanced manufacturing techniques

In the space of eight years, the IBM Havant plant near Portsmouth has increased its turnover fourfold, without needing to increase factory area or take on a single extra employee. What is the key to Havant's success? The answer lies in the use of three major initiatives in manufacturing techniques: computer integrated manufacturing, **quality assurance** and **quality control** methods and **'just in time'** stock control.

The first opportunity to implement all these techniques on one production line came with the introduction of a new disc file storage system, used in the IBM intermediate range of products. Each of these new disc files has a storage capacity which is equivalent to 1,370 paperback novels! Assembly takes place in a 'Class 100 clean room', where conditions are cleaner than an operating theatre. The discs can be very easily damaged, so robots are used for the later stages of assembly.

The key to Havant's success was that it integrated the whole production process right from the start. Production engineers were involved early on at the design stage, so that the product, the layout of the production line and tooling could all be designed together. Computer integrated manufacturing therefore works well at Havant because the plant streamlined their processes first, then computerised them.

Havant realised that if it was to achieve its eventual aim of **zero defects** in terms of standards of quality, traditional quality control through inspection at the end of the production process was not enough. Prevention is better than detection! Havant decided, therefore, to introduce a quality assurance scheme to get quality right at the outset. Most of the parts now come from reliable **certified suppliers**.

Class 100 clean room at IBM Havant

The 'just in time' method was adopted in order to streamline the assembly process. Operators on the production line have the authority to stop the line and request parts, which are delivered automatically only *when needed*. Knock-on benefits of this system are numerous. The tying-up of capital in large amounts of stock has gone. More importantly, less storage space is needed, releasing more space for manufacturing. As workers have more control over the production process, job satisfaction has increased.

The environment – can firms meet the clean technology challenge?

There was a time when green was simply another colour. But when the UK's Green Party leapt from nowhere to win a hefty 15 per cent of the votes cast in the 1989 Euro-Elections, even the most hardened sceptics were forced to concede that the depth of public support for environmental causes was not a passing fad – as concern mounted during the 1980s over issues such as global warming, acid rain, toxic waste and the destruction of the tropical rain forests, it became clear that a new breed of green consumer had emerged.

In the scramble to reflect the new green mood, some manufacturers began to make wildly exaggerated claims for their products. At one time, everything from lead-free petrol to fly-spray was labelled 'ozone friendly'. Inevitably, some of these firms were simply jumping on the bandwagon.

Nevertheless, there were an increasing number of companies who had begun to manufacture products or provide services which were genuinely 'green'. Many of the UK's leading companies have also shown that they are well prepared to meet the clean technology challenge into the 1990s and beyond.

ICI has developed a group of hydrogen-based gases which are designed to replace the chlorine-based CFCs as refrigerant gases. This is a particularly important development in view of the role that CFCs play in depleting the vital ozone layer which protects the earth from harmful ultraviolet rays – one atom of chlorine can wipe out a staggering 100,000 ozone molecules. On top of this, CFCs also contribute to global warming. In fact, as 'greenhouse gases' they have a potential impact 20,000 times greater than carbon dioxide, on a molecule by molecule basis, though carbon dioxide is actually implicated more strongly in global warming purely because it is released in greater quantities.

The advances made by companies such as IBM in phasing out the CFCs that were previously used in their production processes take on even greater significance in the light of these facts. IBM had been using CFCs as solvents to wash their electronic circuit boards. Engineers at their Greenock plant in Scotland discovered, after experimenting with different methods, that washing the boards in soap and water and then drying them in warm air would do the job just as well. Companies such as The BOC Group have launched schemes to recover CFCs from old appliances in order to stop them being discharged into the environment.

Another group of companies is concerned with developing methods to dispose of waste safely. Haden MacLellan converts toxic industrial paint sludge into dried powder to make paint and industrial filler for cars. Simon Engineering have developed a new method of sewage treatment which turns sewage sludge into an inert compost that is safe to use as a soil fertiliser. The process is likely to be widely adopted, especially in view of the announcement by the Government that it intends to outlaw the dumping of sewage sludge at sea from 1998.

Johnson Matthey is one of only four companies in the world to produce catalytic converters for cars. These clean up exhaust emissions by converting harmful gases into less harmful carbon dioxide, nitrogen and water vapour. It is a market that has boomed from 1993, when EC regulations made it compulsory for converters to be fitted to all new cars.

Nor have these environmental initiatives been confined purely to manufacturing. Amongst the major supermarket chains Tesco has been at the forefront of the green movement with its 'Tesco Cares' campaign. The label is used on products ranging from phosphate-free cleaning agents to recycled tissues. Tesco has also provided space for over 150 bottle banks and around 60 paper banks and is running trial schemes for the reclamation of aluminium and plastics. The company has pioneered a comprehensive labelling policy, sells a range of organic produce in many of its stores and abstains from animal testing on own-label goods. It sells lead-free petrol at all its filling stations and has also converted the company car fleet to run on lead-free petrol wherever possible. Other supermarket chains have since followed Tesco's lead and introduced similar measures in their stores.

In general, consumers have now come to expect that the products they buy should be ecologically sound. However, some of the products which have been widely regarded as environmentally friendly have recently come under attack. Critics point out that some recycled toilet papers are made of scarce top grade paper which ought instead to be used for high quality products such as stationery.

Ecobalance research can be useful in cases such as this. It involves weighing up the environmental impact of a product at every stage of its life from the extraction of raw materials needed for its manufacture through to its eventual disposal as waste. The analysis can sometimes yield unexpected findings. Ecobalance research carried out in Germany discovered that in terms of the balance between energy efficiency, manufacturing pollution and recycling, it was better to use plastic bags sparingly than to use recycled paper bags.

The whole environmental debate focuses increasingly on the crucial question of who should bear the cost of a cleaner environment – consumers, companies, governments? Some companies have spent considerable sums on making improvements where necessary, but in some cases environmental awareness has had to be balanced by commercial considerations.

According to David Chambers and Elaine Chester in an article which appeared in *Business Magazine* in August 1990, 'Earlier this year, the government revealed it was not going ahead, in full, with a £2 billion programme to fit sulphur dioxide filtering equipment to 12,000 megawatts of coal-fired generating capacity. Instead, National Power is going ahead with de-sulphurisation only at Drax in North Yorkshire, covering 4,000 megawatts of capacity.' The changes have been influenced by fears that the privatisation of the electricity companies would be seriously affected if the industry were to be burdened with extensive clean-up costs. Instead, the generating authorities are looking at alternative energy sources such as gas, which make no contribution to acid rain, as well as cleaner types of coal with a lower sulphur content.

Clearly, the solving of environmental problems poses many dilemmas. But an aspect of the debate that is often overlooked is that it pays to be green. The market for environmentally friendly products and technologies is estimated to be worth between £100 billion and £150 billion. This is apart from the estimated £200 million which is invested in the shares of companies with a good record on ethical and environmental issues. Those with impeccable green credentials are also likely to fare better when recruiting from the shrinking pool of young job applicants.

There is also a growing realisation amongst companies that improvements made on environmental grounds can often produce considerable cost savings. 3M, whose interests range from Post-It notes to abrasives, discovered that since launching their 'Pollution Prevention Pays' programme in 1975 the amount of pollution created by the company has been cut by half, saving an estimated £500 million. The 3P programme, as it is known, is based on the principle that it is easier to prevent pollution in the first place than it is to clean it up afterwards.

A typical scheme at a 3M plant in South Wales, for example, involved changing the backing paper for the abrasive discs made at the plant, so that the abrasive could be hot-melted onto the backing. Not only did the scheme prevent pollution (which had been caused by the solvents previously used to coat the abrasive onto the backing), it also required no capital to set up and saved the company £150,000 a year into the bargain.

Many more firms will need to meet the clean technology challenge. Even those who at present show little concern for the environment are likely to be influenced by the domino effect, whereby larger firms will impose their standards on suppliers by refusing to do business with them unless they meet the right environmental standards.

We, as consumers, may well have to accept a change in our lifestyles, in terms of commuting by car to work, for example. Despite the fact that cars are now more energy efficient and cause less pollution, it is difficult to see how any car can be really 'green'. In any case, the use of lead-free petrol and the fitting of catalytic converters are not the complete answer to the problems posed by car exhaust fumes. Whilst they may cut the level of emissions per vehicle, the benefits are cancelled out by the vast increase in the total number of vehicles on the road. The Economist Intelligence Unit estimates that there will be 550 million vehicles in the world by the end of the century, which represents a 50 per cent increase in 50 years.

It is debatable whether continued growth, following the pattern of the advanced industrial nations, will be sustainable in the future. James Robertson in his book, *Future Wealth*, points out that according to the Bruntland Report by the World Commission on Environment and Development, 'The current damage to the global environment is being perpetrated by a quarter of the world's population of 5 billion. Given its probable population of 10–14 billion by 2050, and the urge for the rest of the world to mirror what it sees as the magnificent standard of living we enjoy in the West, the result would be an impact 20 to 30 times greater than now upon our already protesting ecology.

FINAL ACTIVITY

CEE DEE Sounds: production line simulation

THE BRIEF

The aim of this exercise is to simulate the organisation of a production line during one shift in a compact disc factory. As the market is fairly new, each factory has received the same order for this operating period, which is for its maximum production.

Your group now represents one factory unit of six people and you will need to fulfil orders from three record companies. The orders must be completed as quickly as possible, but without compromising quality. Due to a shortage of production capacity, all good products are being snapped up by the buyer from WH Jones.

START UP

Before the 40-minute production period starts, each factory unit will have 15 minutes in which they need to:

1 Appoint one production manager/cum salesperson.
2 Choose a company name.
3 Read the manufacturing instructions and operating conditions.
4 Put in the first order of raw materials.
5 Plan how production will be organised in terms of worker organisation, stock control, quality control and management. Each unit will also need to plan which orders to deal with first.

The buyer from WH Jones and the supplier from Plas-Tec Ltd need to be appointed too.

OPERATING CONDITIONS

* Raw materials needed for manufacture can be bought from the suppliers, Plas-Tec Ltd.
* Each group can order as much as they want of white card at £1 per sheet and coloured paper at £2 per sheet.
* Requests to buy materials from Plas-Tec Ltd will be dealt with in the order received and delays may occur.
* Factories left with unwanted stock at the end of the operating period will only be able to value it at half the purchase price.
* Buyers will only accept delivery in batches of four CDs and will deal with salespeople in the order in which they visit.
* If the buyer finds one substandard CD (e.g. one that is poorly cut out or with unclear logos) in a batch offered by a salesperson, the whole batch will be rejected.
* The buyer from WH Jones will pay the prices shown in the order details table.
* Partly finished batches of 'work in progress' will be valued at half sales value.
* A complete order fulfilled with 'zero defects' will earn a bonus of 10 per cent from the buyer.
* Assembly line workers will be paid £4 each and the manager £6 for the operating period.

MANUFACTURING INSTRUCTIONS

At the start, each group will be given a set of manufacturing equipment. The compact discs are made by cutting a circle of 12 cm diameter, out of white A4 card and sticking a circular label of 5 cm diameter, cut from A4 coloured paper, in the centre. Labels must be in the right colour and marked in the centre with the appropriate logo for each company, as shown in the order details table. Each factory unit can choose the name of a song and group for each batch of CDs that they make and add these to the labels above the logo.

Manufacturing equipment for each group

2 pairs of scissors   1 ruler
1 stick of paper glue   2 pencils
1 compass   1 black felt-tip pen

Name of recording company	Company logo	Colour of label	Number of discs ordered	Price paid per disc (£)
AMI	AMI	Red	16	7
Becca	*Becca*	Blue	8	8
Firips	Firips	Green	4	9

	Team 1	Team 2	Team 3	Team 4
Value of total sales (from buyers' records)				
Value of unsold stock (half purchase price)				
Total revenue				
Fixed costs	£70	£70	£70	£70
Material costs (from store's record)				
Labour costs				
Total costs				
Total operating profit or loss				

Plas-Tec stores record

		Team 1	Team 2	Team 3	Team 4
White card @ £1 sheet	Order 1				
	Order 2				
	Order 3				
	Order 4				
Coloured paper @ £2 sheet	Order 1				
	Order 2				
	Order 3				
	Order 4				
Total material costs					

WH Jones buyers' records

		Team 1	Team 2	Team 3	Team 4
AMI @ £7 each	Batch 1				
	Batch 2				
	Batch 3				
	Batch 4				
BECCA @ £8 each	Batch 1				
	Batch 2				
Firips @ £9 each	Batch 1				
Total Sales					

Discussion points

1 Did a division of labour emerge in each factory group?
2 Did the production manager actually plan and supervise?
3 Were there delays in waiting for stock or was capital tied up in over-ordered stock?
4 How was quality control ensured?
5 Were many batches rejected by the buyer for being substandard?
6 Did groups have an operating strategy, such as going for the cheaper 'volume' end of the market or the more expensive end?

Personnel

IN ASSOCIATION WITH 🅣🅢🅑

When Tom Peters and Robert Waterman were researching their book, *In Search of Excellence*, the conclusions they arrived at were not at all what they had expected. Rather than sophisticated systems of management and control being behind the success of their 'excellent' American companies, it was proven time and time again to be the employees' attitudes that made the difference. Do the firms with employees that perform consistently well have anything in common?

Although company styles vary, what is certain is that all successful firms possess the ability to tap the potential of their employees so that people identify strongly with company goals and are willing to channel all their energies and enthusiasm into achieving them. This degree of commitment is not achieved purely because they have concentrated on recruiting high fliers. In fact, quite 'ordinary' people produce exceptional performances in these progressive firms. Their employees appear, in general, to show commitment and feel that the company is a good one to work for. So how do these firms encourage such motivation?

Successful firms recruit carefully, train their employees well and recognise their achievements, adopt caring welfare policies, create climates which motivate people and have a cooperative company culture which minimises industrial conflict.

HOW TO STOP THE COMPANY STIFLING PEOPLE AND STRANGLING PROFITS

So reads the challenging subtitle of Robert Townsend's book, *Up the Organisation*.

In the 13 years prior to Townsend taking over as chairman, Avis Rent-a-Car never made a profit, yet three years later the sales had grown from $30 million to $75 million. The following excerpts of his views on different ways of treating people give some clues as to the reasons behind this remarkable turnaround.

On people

'Most people in big companies today are administered not led. They are treated as personnel not people. Get to know your people. What they do well, what they enjoy doing, what their weaknesses and strengths are and what they want and need to get from their job.'

Message to chief executives

'Certainly today, no meeting of the high and mighty is complete until someone polishes the conventional wisdom, "Our big trouble today is getting enough good people ..."

This is crystal clear nonsense. Your people aren't lazy and incompetent. They just look that way. They're beaten by all the overlapping and interlocking policies, rules and systems encrusting your company.'

On promotion

'Most managements complain about the lack of able people and go outside to fill key positions. Nonsense. I use the rule of 50 per cent. Try to find somebody inside the company with a record of success (in any area) and with an appetite for the job. If they look like 50 per cent of what you need, give them the job. In six months they'll have grown the other 50 per cent and everybody will be satisfied.'

Firms need to recruit carefully, so that they can find the right people for their requirements. If their recruitment procedures are inefficient, staff turnover will be high, with all the resulting waste of time, energy and administrative costs. Worse still, the people who are poor appointments can stay on and perform badly, blocking the career path of people who deserve to be promoted.

Recruiting the right people

ACTIVITY

Analysing the recruitment process

THE RECRUITMENT CAMPAIGN AT J SIMPSON LTD

'We're so short staffed in the Data Centre, we're going to have to take on another trainee computer operator', said Neil Morris, the computer systems controller.

'But before we do that,' replied Linda Groves, the personnel manager, 'are you sure you really need to appoint someone? It's become so expensive to recruit externally. There's also the cost of management time and the new salary which has to be paid.'

'I know, but I've done my manpower planning and the workload for the department means I definitely need one person now. I'll also need a manager to replace Alan when he retires at Easter, though we could probably recruit internally for his job.'

'OK. So have you done a job description giving details of what the job involves?'

'Yes, it's here. I've also worked out a more detailed job specification. I reckon we want someone with A-levels and a bit of experience of working with computers, though we would obviously train them. Oh yes, and a clean driving licence. Also, personal qualities like the ability to work under pressure and to work well in a team are essential.'

'I'm sure we'll get someone good. So I'll put an advert in the local papers next week and also contact the Job Centre and Careers Office. I might give one or two of the local careers teachers a ring as well. Now, what do we need to say about the remuneration package in the advert?'

'Well, I was thinking of offering a salary of £15,000 a year. The five weeks' paid holiday, free staff restaurant and sports club facilities ought to tempt quite a few people. Though the company pension scheme and free life assurance might seem a bit far off at that age! You'll let me know once the application forms start coming in, so we can draw up a shortlist for the interviews?'

1   What are the stages in the recruitment process?
2   What other forms of external recruitment might be used if the manager's job needs to be advertised?

ACTIVITY

Evaluating Paul's interview

'THE JOB'S AS GOOD AS MINE'

'If it hadn't been for that 9 o'clock bus being late, I'd have been all right', thought Paul, as he ran up the steps of J Simpson Ltd's building and dashed up to the reception desk.

'Excuse me,' he panted, 'I've got an interview at 9.45 a.m. for the trainee computer operator's job.'

'Oh yes. Mr Wilkins, isn't it?' said the receptionist. 'They've just rung down. It's Room 406, up on the fourth floor.'

'I suppose I should have taken Dad up on his offer of a lift into town this morning', thought Paul. 'But then again, I'd have had to get up really early and would have just been hanging around here. Never mind, I'm only 15 minutes late.'

Trying to straighten his tie and flatten his hair, which seemed to be all over the place after his run from the bus stop, he missed the sign for room 406 and went the wrong way down the corridor. When he found the right room at last, Paul knocked on the door and peered nervously round.

'Do come in, Mr Wilkins. I'm Linda Groves, the personnel manager, and this is Neil Morris, the computer systems controller.'

Sitting down, Paul put his jacket on the back of the chair and moved a bit nearer the desk.

'Oh yes, do make yourself comfortable', said Linda Groves. 'Did you have a good journey?'

'Not too bad, thanks. Except that the bus was a bit late and then I had trouble finding the room.'

'I see. Now, I understand you're doing A-levels at present. Can you tell us what made you apply for this post?'

'Well, I wanted to get a job and earn a bit of money, rather than going on to college for another three years. It's not too far for me to travel here and my Dad says Simpson's is a very good company to work for.'

'That's very interesting. Tell me, which subjects do you enjoy most at school?' asked Linda, glancing at the papers in front of her.

'Computer Science is the only thing I like at school. We've got a really good teacher. Mr Robinson's great. He doesn't mind if we have a bit of a laugh now and then. Geography's quite interesting, but Economics is a bit boring at times. All those graphs and statistics! Still, it's not too bad, I suppose. Only another term to go!'

Encouraged by his progress so far, when asked about his involvement in other school activities Paul went on to add that he played rugby for the school in the third year and always went along to the sixth-form discos.

'And what do you like doing in your spare time?' asked Linda.

'I like watching TV and listening to music mostly. I don't do rugby any more. All those practices after school got a bit much in the end.'

'Now tell me, Paul,' said Neil Morris as he leant forward, 'What computer applications did your course cover?'

'Er, well. Let me see. We did spreadsheets, databases, word processing, all that kind of thing. Oh, and we did quite a lot on systems. We also did a kind of project. That wasn't bad. It was difficult to think of something to do at first. Anyway, Mr Robinson found me a topic to do in the end.'

As the interview went on, Paul felt more relaxed, so when Neil asked him why he wanted a career in computing he was able to reply confidently, 'You see, I've always wanted a nice steady job and I've heard you can earn really good money in computing if you get on.'

He was a bit surprised when Linda asked if he had a driving licence. She said it was mentioned in the advertisement and in the job profile that they had sent out to all candidates. He could not remember noticing that at all. But it was always such a rush these days, what with homework, working at the local supermarket and going out with Jane. Still, never mind, he thought he had carried it off well by saying he was quite prepared to start taking lessons.

'Is there anything you would like to ask us about the job?' asked Linda finally.

'No, not really. I can always find out everything I need to know later on. Oh! It is five weeks' holiday, isn't it?'

'Yes, that's right. Well, it's been interesting talking to you, Paul. We will be contacting all the applicants in due course. Thank you for coming.'

As Paul stood up to say goodbye, he felt quite pleased with himself, feeling sure that the job was as good as his already.

1   As a group, discuss Paul's performance in terms of:
    a) Preparation for the interview.
    b) Behaviour during the interview.
    c) Reasons for wanting the job revealed by his answers.
    d) Attitudes to work, degree of initiative shown and likely commitment to the company, as revealed by his answers.
2   In pairs, with each person taking a turn at being Paul, role play how 'you' think Paul should have handled the interview.

DO INTERVIEWS WORK?

Paul's performance in this interview was clearly inadequate, though partly a result of his inexperience. But just how good *are* interviews at getting the right person for the job? A growing body of evidence suggests that traditional interviewing may be far less effective than people like to think.

Research has shown that interviewers tend to form an initial impression within the first five minutes or so of the candidate walking through the door, and from then on spend their time searching for additional information to substantiate their hunches. Worse still, research has also shown that a candidate rated best by one interviewer may be rated poorest by another. So a candidate's chances of success may largely depend on who interviews him or her on the day! There is also a danger of interviewers placing too much emphasis on one or two criteria they have identified as being important, and ignoring evidence relating to other qualities the candidate may possess.

As interviews are still the single most important method of selection and seem to be here to stay, it is vitally important to improve their effectiveness. To this end, many companies such as ICI, British Airways and National Westminster Bank are now using **situational interviewing** methods. This is where candidates are presented with a series of hypothetical events based on situations that might arise in the job they are applying for and are asked how they would respond. Their answers are then compared with what people who are already in the company and are known to be performing similar jobs effectively would do in those situations.

This technique has already proved highly successful in selecting people with management potential. Clearly, situational interviewing can prove invaluable for effective recruitment in that it lessens the danger of interviewers relying on their gut feelings.

Is appraisal necessary?

In most large firms, staff appraisal, where the employees individually discuss their progress with their immediate managers, is carried out once or twice a year. Appraisal is usually done in order to discuss how well employees are doing and how they can improve their work. The assessment of strengths and weaknesses is also useful in determining where further training may be needed and whether employees are ready for promotion. In some firms, the appraisal determines their salary increase for the year.

These advantages have prompted more and more firms to introduce appraisal schemes, sometimes based on the use of a standard appraisal form. Clearly, formal appraisal will only be useful in situations where employees do not see the criticism as being destructive and where the managers do not shy away from making unfavourable appraisals where necessary. In any case, formal appraisals should not be seen as a substitute for continuous feedback during the year.

Is training important?

In an article in *British Business*, the DTI's magazine, it is claimed that each year in Germany two or three times more fitters, electricians and building craftsworkers become qualified than in the UK and five times as many clerical workers. As Brian Nickson of the Institute of Training and Development (ITD) points out, 'If companies are to keep up with new technology, become more competitive abroad, attract good quality staff and increase their profits, they must make a real commitment to training.'

How, then, can training help firms achieve these benefits? At a time when the pace of technological change is so rapid, workers must be retrained to learn the new skills needed and taught to be flexible enough to adapt to further changes in their working lives. Clearly, trained workers will produce a greater quantity and better quality of work than untrained workers. The existence of a good training programme within a company is likely both to attract good staff and to keep them, as people like to feel that they are improving their skills so that they can progress in their careers. On a practical level, training in health and safety is absolutely essential. It follows that an effective training programme which leads to improved performance for employees and boosts morale must also increase company profits.

Traditionally, training has been **on-the-job training**, the simplest form of which is learning by 'sitting next to Nellie'. This can be effective, though training by an experienced worker may be inefficient and could result in bad habits being learnt. However, the fact that most academic training for professional jobs, such as teaching, also requires a period of on-the-job training before the qualification is finally awarded, is a recognition of the importance of practical experience.

Off-the-job training, becoming increasingly popular with the decline of apprentice training, is when training is given by specialist instructors in the firms' own training schools or in colleges. The main advantage is that employees can learn faster by following a carefully planned training programme than by learning in the working environment.

In recent years, many firms have adopted **computer based training (CBT)** methods, where trainees work through learning programs written specifically for the firm. Michelin Tyre Plc, for example, have found employees much prefer this type of training once they have overcome their initial fear of operating the equipment. The Royal Mail also found that 'by taking an active role in their own training and by learning at their own pace, people retain 40 per cent more information than they would with any other training method.'

What motivates people?

When people's needs are not met in their job, complaints and fatigue increase, productivity drops, absenteeism is likely to rise, and in extreme cases even violence and sabotage can occur. It is important, therefore, for firms to know what motivates people in order to ensure their needs are met. Various writers have tried to identify these motivating factors.

FW TAYLOR (1911)

Writing in the early part of the century, Taylor's methods were founded on the basis that 'what workmen want from their employers beyond anything else is high wages'. He argued that tasks, even simple ones like shovelling, could be broken down into smaller components and analysed, and then unnecessary or inefficient processes could be removed. After scientific study of the job, the correct output which workers should achieve in a day could be decided on. Workers who then met this productivity target should be paid much higher wages.

Though his principles later became widely adopted as the basis of **work study** methods, he was severely criticised, even in his own time, for seeing money as the main motivating factor and for reducing workers to the level of efficient machines. In all fairness, however, few employers have been willing to implement all his ideas fully, like having no limit to the amount highly productive workers can earn.

E MAYO (1933)

Mayo's research has been influential in revealing that the general ethos and values held by informal social groups at work are more important in determining productivity levels than are other changes.

In the famous Hawthorne experiment, a group of workers were segregated in order to observe the effect on output and morale of various changes. As each improvement was introduced, such as incentive payments, rest pauses, shorter hours and refreshments, productivity rose. Then it was decided to return to the original conditions of a six-day, 48-hour week, with no incentives, no rest pauses and no refreshments. Expecting a fall in output, researchers were amazed when productivity soared to the highest levels ever reached!

Though it seemed a mystery then, Mayo's later explanation was that by this time a tightly knit social group had formed, who benefited from the attention shown by researchers and who worked to achieve the output levels they thought the researchers expected. The research has stimulated an increasing tendency for production to be organised in small groups and encouraged managers to realise the importance of praise, attention and good communications in getting workers to identify and work towards company goals.

AH MASLOW (1943)

Maslow argued that people seek to satisfy a hierarchy of needs, with lower-level needs being satisfied before higher-level needs. (See diagram on p. 10.) With increased living standards this century, lower-level needs such as those for physical survival and safety tend to have been satisfied. Firms who now wish to persuade their employees to work harder can only do so by offering them the opportunity to fulfil higher-level needs. These include the satisfaction of social needs (belonging to a group), esteem needs (being highly regarded) and the need for self-fulfilment (gaining satisfaction by being creative, for instance).

D MCGREGOR (1960)

Theories like Taylor's, which view employees as disliking work and which emphasise high wages and strict supervision as the best way of ensuring maximum productivity, are based on certain assumptions about what workers are like. McGregor called these assumptions *Theory X*. Instead, his own *Theory Y* is based on assumptions that people find work natural, that they exercise self-control in meeting objectives to which they are committed, that they will not only accept but actively seek responsibility and will want to take part in decision making.

The implications of McGregor's theories are far-reaching. Clearly, firms need to create Theory Y climates and working conditions so that workers can motivate themselves, with managers performing a supportive role rather than a traditional controlling role.

F HERZBERG (1966)

Herzberg developed his theory of incentives by asking a sample of employees what made them happy or unhappy at work. On this basis, he identified *hygiene* or *maintenance factors*, such as adequate pay and working conditions, as not being **motivators**. If these are inadequate, workers will fight to have them improved, but they do not actually encourage people to work harder. The *real* motivators were factors relating to the job itself, like the opportunity for achievement, recognition and advancement. The chance to exercise creativity and take on responsibility were also important.

Contrary to Taylor's early ideas, these later writers have argued that people are motivated by many needs and do not work for money alone. In fact, it can often be seen that people's whole identity stems from the work they do and the organisation they work for. The evidence that work is a psychological need is borne out by the effects of unemployment on people, many of whom report a loss of identity and esteem and a general feeling of alienation from society.

ACTIVITY

The needs fulfilled by different jobs

I Identify which higher-order needs, such as the need for esteem and recognition, or for self-fulfilment through the chance to exercise creativity or take on responsibility, are likely to be fulfilled in the following jobs:

Rock star	Cabinet minister	Airline pilot
Barrister	First division footballer	Music composer
Surgeon	Train driver	Fashion designer

2 Which needs would you expect your future job to fulfil?

Hodder & Stoughton Educational © Permission to photocopy for classroom use only.

Discussion point

Do you think unemployed people suffer through not being able to fulfil any of these needs through a job?

CASE STUDY

Kalmar – production on a human scale

In the mid-1970s, the Kalmar car works in Sweden was hailed as Volvo's answer to the labour problems associated with traditional assembly line production methods, and still provides a classic example of production on a human scale. The high rates of absenteeism and high labour turnover being experienced generally were symptoms of the trend everywhere for production line jobs to become boring and repetitive as a result of increasingly specialised division of labour. Not surprisingly, workers found it almost impossible to take a pride in their jobs and in the finished product, when all they were doing was one small operation in the production process. Unlike Britain, Sweden suffers from a labour shortage, so Volvo faced great difficulties in recruiting labour. As jobs were freely available, workers were reluctant to choose assembly line work.

The unique design of its new plant to produce the Volvo 760s was, ironically, a step nearer to the way cars were originally made in the past, when they were made by teams of skilled workers in specialist workshops. Instead of the conventional production line organisation, teams of workers at Kalmar were made responsible for assembling one complete section of the car – for example, one team would assemble the whole steering system. The 15 to 20 operators who comprised each team could decide how the work was to be divided up between themselves and could control the pace of their 40-minute cycles. Changes such as these and the fact that teams could decide when to have their breaks went a long way towards breaking up the monotony of the work. Each team was also allocated their own area of the building, with their own entrance, changing room and coffee area.

The organisation of the work along these lines was designed to relieve boredom, increase job satisfaction, foster teamwork and enable workers to take a pride in the finished product.

As hoped, the problems management thought would be solved by the new system largely disappeared, though the initiative was not without its problems. The initial capital investment was far higher than for a traditional car plant and, although quality has improved, productivity is generally lower. However, there is no doubt that the human lessons learnt at Kalmar will act as a catalyst for change in traditionally organised assembly plants everywhere.

Discussion points

1 Should companies organise production to ensure worker satisfaction or to gain high productivity?

2 Are the two aims in fact incompatible?

3 What factors might influence companies' eventual decision?

Do pay and incentives motivate?

Traditional payment systems based on **time rates** (i.e. the number of hours worked) are necessary for many jobs – where output cannot be measured, where quality is so important the job should not be hurried, or where the speed of work cannot be controlled by the workers. With this system, workers cannot earn more if they work harder.

The **payment by results** method is often used for production workers whose output can be measured. Here, workers can earn more if they work harder.

Much research since Herzberg has confirmed the importance of firms creating the right conditions where workers can satisfy their higher needs and thus work harder. Important though this is, many companies today also encourage motivation by operating **incentive schemes** which involve a merit award being paid for extra performance.

Merit awards should, however, not be regularly paid, but awarded on appraisal. Otherwise they become expected as a right, not a reward. As Robert Townsend also points out, in *Up the Organisation*, 'Rewarding outstanding performances is important. Much more neglected is the equally important need to make sure that the underachievers don't get rewarded. This is more painful, so it doesn't get done very often.'

An extension of the incentive principle is **profit sharing**, where employees get a bonus according to the profit made by the company, sometimes linked to the issue of shares. The John Lewis Partnership introduced a profit-sharing scheme as long ago as 1929. Apart from the motivating aspects of such schemes, they do also have the advantage of encouraging workers to identify with the company.

Does participation in decision making motivate?

Much research has been done which shows that where workers participate in decision making, motivation is enhanced through them becoming more involved and committed and feeling that their opinions matter. On a more basic level, it is recognised that when workers' opinions influence a particular course of action being taken, they are far more determined to go all out to make that course of action work, rather than if it is just someone else's decision handed down for them to carry out.

Worker participation can take place on different levels. At one end of the scale are **consultative committees**, found in many companies. Worker representatives elected to these committees can influence decisions concerning a wide range of everyday issues affecting the company. At the other end of the scale, in some companies **worker representatives** are appointed to the board and have a chance to influence major policy decisions. However, critics of this system argue that workers are not capable of making any long-term policy decisions.

Some European firms have avoided this problem by adopting a dual system. This consists of a top-level board which is equivalent to the traditional board of directors and makes overall policy decisions, and a second-level board, including worker representatives, which is responsible for day-to-day management.

The role of trade unions today

Trade unions began during the early stages of the Industrial Revolution, in the late eighteenth century and the early nineteenth century. They were a result of workers in factories, mines and mills, who were paid extremely low wages and endured harsh working conditions, realising that employers would be more likely to take notice of their grievances if they joined together as groups and voiced them rather than trying to speak out as individuals.

There are currently 268 unions in the UK with just over 9 million members, of which 40 per cent are women. About 35 per cent of the working population in Great Britain belongs to a union, and 34 per cent of non-manual workers belong to a trade union.

There are four types of union:

- **General unions**, which represent workers in a range of industries.
- **Craft unions**, which represent workers from a group of industries who share a particular skill.
- **Industrial unions**, which represent workers in a particular industry whatever their skill.
- **White collar unions**, which represent non-manual workers.

Trade unions negotiate with employers by means of **collective bargaining** to improve pay, working conditions and job security. To improve the effectiveness of collective bargaining some industries operate a **closed shop**, where employers have an agreement with one or more trade unions that only union members will be employed.

Most unions are now affiliated to the **Trade Union Congress (TUC)**, founded in 1968. Many employers' associations have also been formed in recent years, most of which now belong to the **Confederation of British Industry (CBI)**, whose role for employers is basically the same as the TUC's is for the unions.

In recent years, the government has become more involved in industrial relations. The **Advisory, Conciliation and Arbitration Service (ACAS)**, founded in 1975, was set up to encourage more collective bargaining agreements and to offer help and advice to unions and employers when negotiations break down. If a dispute goes into **arbitration** and ACAS is called in it will take into account every aspect of the dispute and make a decision, which both sides then have to abide by.

WHAT DO PEOPLE THINK OF TRADE UNIONS?

Trade union membership had declined in recent years from its peak of 12 million members in 1979, partly due to rising unemployment and partly due to changing patterns of employment.

There is no doubt that trade unions have received adverse media publicity in recent years. Critics argue that trade unions make excessive wage claims that are primarily responsible for inflation and for pricing workers out of jobs. Criticisms have also been made of undemocratic elections, and in order to overcome this charge unions now have to elect their leaders by secret ballot.

Others argue that unions have become too powerful and should have their 'wings clipped'. Some think that workers in vital industries such as power and transport should not be allowed to join unions because of the possible effect on public safety if they went on strike. Workers at GCHQ, the government communications and surveillance centre, are no longer allowed to be members of any union.

Another charge frequently levelled at unions is that they undermine the competitiveness of British industry because of restrictive practices and opposition to technological progress. However, a survey by ACAS in 1988 of 650 employers showed that 'the presence of trade unions has not appeared to inhibit the introduction of new working practices'.

Supporters of trade unions argue that they are essential for protecting the interests of employees who might otherwise get a raw deal from powerful employers or in industries which are declining and where redundancies are highly likely. Unskilled workers can be in a particularly weak position.

Unions played an active part in persuading the government to pass the Health and Safety at Work Act. They also offer a range of personal services, legal advice, training, protection against unfair dismissal, and accident and sickness benefits, and can attempt to influence government policy by political lobbying, particularly through the TUC.

There have also been a small number (between 150 and 200 companies) of new-style agreements signed between employers and unions, involving single-union deals and no-strike clauses. Their importance for attracting foreign investment cannot be overestimated at a time when many international companies still perceive Britain's record of industrial unrest with suspicion. Ford's recent bid to build a single-union plant in Dundee failed when the unions objected on the grounds that the deal would undermine existing agreements at other Ford plants. An estimated 1,500 much-needed jobs were lost. Ford built the plant in Cadiz in Spain instead.

Some observers argue that these new-style agreements, such as the one at Toshiba UK's plant in Plymouth (see the case study later in this chapter), point the way forward for a new era of industrial relations in Britain.

ACTIVITY

Attitude battery towards the role of trade unions

On a copy of the table below, list the advantages and disadvantages of trade unions. Use the points mentioned in the text and any other points you can think of. You should have 10 statements in all.

	Statements	Agree strongly	Agree	Neither agree nor disagree	Disagree	Strongly disagree
Advantages						
Disadvantages						

Put a tick in the box which sums up your attitude towards each statement. What does your attitude battery reveal about your underlying attitudes to trade unions?

Hodder & Stoughton Educational © Permission to photocopy for classroom use only.

CASE STUDY

Toshiba (UK) – new-style industrial relations

At the Toshiba electronics factory in Plymouth, both management and union were recently celebrating the anniversary of the signing, in 1981, of Britain's first single-union, strike-free agreement. Since then, between 150 and 200 companies around the country, have followed Toshiba's lead and signed similar deals.

Aimed at boosting production and ending disputes, the single-union, strike-free deal at Toshiba has revolutionised the traditional 'them and us' confrontational view of industrial relations. To what extent has the deal been successful and what were the underlying principles on which it was founded?

The new-style philosophy was born out of the closure of the old Rank television factory which Toshiba had run as a joint venture with Rank from 1978 and which was making heavy losses. When the modernised factory was re-opened in 1981 under Toshiba's sole ownership, with 300 of the original 2,600 workers, it was seen as an opportunity to start afresh using the best of Japanese and European practices.

The central features of the agreement with the AEEU (Amalgamated Engineering and Electrical Union) was the setting up of a company advisory board, made up of elected representatives from all levels of the company, who meet once a month to discuss all issues affecting the company.

Once proposals actually started to be put into practice, the advisory board began to be seen in a different light: workers realised that it was not some sort of management 'con trick' and that if they had a valid suggestion to make, it would be considered seriously. People are not afraid to speak their minds now and discussions can get very heated at times!

Meeting of the company advisory board at Toshiba, Plymouth

In the event of a deadlock, which has yet to happen, both management and the single engineering union have agreed to abide by an independent arbitrator's decision. This in effect constitutes a no-strike agreement.

Perhaps the single-union, no-strike deal would have been seen as one-sided and would never have been accepted by the workforce, if Toshiba had not also introduced from the start the concept of 'single status'. Everyone, from management to shop-floor workers, is employed under the same working conditions. All 1,000 workers, or 'members' as they are known, work the same 39-hour week, eat in the same restaurant and have the same sickness, pension and holiday entitlement. All workers are expected to be flexible in terms of their job descriptions. Senior managers, including George Williams, the managing director, can be seen around the factory wearing their blue uniform company jackets and eating with everyone else in the restaurant. They do not have separate offices, just a desk along with 100 others on the open-plan administration floor.

Workers obviously feel that the removal of divisive management privileges lessens the gap found in the traditional 'them and us' set-up. Generally, there seems to be a more positive attitude around. As the production manager points out, 'We don't get empty fag packets shoved into TV sets, like we used to in the old days'. 'It's not all sweetness and light,' says George Harris, the personnel director, 'but we manage to settle most problems in a civilised way.'

Attitude surveys are conducted to find out what employees think and votes are taken on any changes proposed. A vote to start work at 8.00 a.m. instead of 8.30 a.m., in order to have a four-and-a-half-day week, was carried by 84 per cent of members, but it is typical of Toshiba's personnel policies that the decision will not go ahead until the other 16 per cent have been consulted to find out why they objected.

Absenteeism is a third of what it was in Rank days and production is now the highest of any Toshiba plant outside Japan. There is no doubt that if the plant had not shown that the new-style agreements were working, the multi-million pound investment in a new microwave oven factory, which was added in 1985, would have gone to a Toshiba plant in West Germany instead. The factory now produces air conditioning units.

However, improvements have not arisen effortlessly. Plaques from the Japanese parent company praising the workers' achievements hang in the boardroom. As George Williams points out, 'When we recruit, we look for enthusiasm and commitment above all. We can always train people in terms of expertise, but we can't train them in terms of attitude.'

Discussion points

1 What are the implications of the new-style agreements at Toshiba?

2 How essential is the 'single status' concept to the agreement's success?

Population trends: a demographic time bomb?

The 'demographic time bomb' has been quietly ticking away for some time. Yet despite widespread media attention the issue has given rise to very little public concern. Perhaps largely because, as the experience of history shows, gloomy predictions by experts tend not to be taken very seriously, or at least not until the effects begin to bite and are patently obvious to all.

From now on, though, firms who take no account of the implications of demographic trends when they plan ahead are likely to face great difficulties in recruiting and retaining staff.

So what are the demographic changes taking place in Britain? The most fundamental change is occurring in the numbers of 18 year olds which will, as a result of falling birth rates, have declined by 27 per cent between 1985 and 1995. It follows from this that many of the new entrants and re-entrants to the workforce will thus have to be female.

An Institute of Manpower Studies Survey found that women would account for a staggering 83 per cent of the growth in employment between 1988 and 1995. There has, in any case, been a substantial increase in the numbers of women in employment during the post-war period, from 6.7 million in 1948 to 11.6 million in 1994. This represents a rise of 73 per cent, compared with a 3.5 per cent increase in the numbers of men employed in the same period. Women now account for almost half the workforce.

A third major shift in employment patterns will stem from the increasing numbers of people who want to work part time. Even in 1994, 28 per cent of the total workforce in Britain, and as much as 36 per cent of the services sector, is already working part time. In fact, Britain has by far the largest part-time workforce in Europe.

How, then, can firms prepare for these changes? The options available to them as the pool of school leavers dries up are, in fact, very limited. They can leave their recruitment policies unchanged and hope that they will be able to take on as many young people as before. However, achieving this implies that they will be successful in increasing their own share of the available labour pool at the expense of their competitors.

The fact is only those companies which are able to offer very attractive packages, in terms of salaries and perks as well as working conditions, are likely to maintain their existing recruitment targets. The prime example of a company which has been successful in this respect is Marks and Spencer. With 44,000 sales assistants, Marks and Spencer has built an enviable reputation in the retailing industry for its standards of pay and staff benefits.

Alternatively, firms can try to reduce their staffing levels so that they need fewer new recruits. This can be done by increasing the pace at which automation of manual and semi-skilled jobs and computerisation of clerical jobs is taking place. In addition, getting rid of unnecessary bureaucracy can not only improve the efficiency of their administrative procedures but will invariably also lead to a significant drop in the amount of staff required.

A further option is for firms to recruit from a huge, and as yet largely untapped source – women who have left work in order to have a family. For many employers, this is proving to be the most popular option, as they come to recognise that this group constitutes a vast reservoir of skills and expertise.

Losing trained, experienced women, often at the height of their careers is a great waste to industry. Many more companies will need to follow the lead set by enlightened companies such as TSB who have introduced a variety of measures, as part of their wider equal opportunities scheme, in order to provide support for women who wish to return to work after having a family.

TSB's 'career breaks' scheme allows women to take up to five years away from work, which can be taken as three separate blocks of time. During the career breaks women can attend refresher courses to maintain their skills and keep up-to-date with any changes that have occurred. Whilst on maternity leave, rights to benefits such as mortgage allowances, bonus and profit-share payments as well as pension schemes are all retained. When they do return women can choose to work part time if they wish. Nursery and holiday care schemes, which provide essential support, are being expanded. With a workforce that is 65.5 per cent female, these initiatives are an important part of TSB's continuing success.

It remains to be seen how many UK companies are successful in introducing the changes to work practices which are needed to recruit and retain staff into the 1990s and beyond. What is certain is that few companies will remain unaffected by these changing patterns of demographic trends.

Inevitably, there will be a greater shift in emphasis in the attitude of management towards a more caring ethos, away from the 'hire and fire' mentality which prevailed in the past when labour was more plentiful. This will have profound implications for everything from employment contracts, pay and conditions, pensions and training, to the handling of any disputes which may arise. Since managements will be more concerned to retain staff, they will need to listen more carefully to what their staff want from their working lives. Changing demographic patterns therefore look like having a greater impact on improving employment conditions than the previous decades of employment legislation.

FINAL ACTIVITY

Stylair Ltd: role play exercise in resolving conflict

GENERAL BACKGROUND

Stylair Ltd is a medium-sized private company based in Birmingham. No longer a small family firm, it now employs 430 workers and manufactures a range of electric hairdryers. In the last decade, the company has grown rapidly, profits having increased by 35 per cent each year. This rapid growth has been achieved by Stylair's strategy of supplying well-designed products aimed at the middle range of the market. In recent years, they have experienced considerable competition from other UK manufacturers and have tried to combat this by developing export markets and by keeping costs down.
During its growth, Stylair has experienced no industrial relations problems, though recently some of the workforce have been expressing a few grievances.

BACKGROUND TO THE DISPUTE

Stylair's managing director, Andrew Whittaker, keeps a regular eye on the levels of overtime worked. In his last meeting with the production manager, Mike Hutchings, he mentioned his concern that the level of overtime worked by the maintenance team of six men had been rather high during the last six months. He queried why so much overtime had been done and asked Mike to check that overtime was not being abused.

The following morning, Mike called George Collins, the maintenance supervisor, into his office and told him that the company wanted to clamp down on unnecessary overtime. From now on, overtime would not be allowed without Mike's personal authorisation. George replied that the maintenance men would not like this, as they had come to depend on a certain amount of overtime in their take-home pay. Besides, some machines could only be repaired outside normal working hours.

At lunch that day, George informed his men that management had decided that from now on overtime would no longer be worked. After a heated discussion in the works canteen, the men went back to work after lunch, still complaining angrily about the new ruling.

Ten days later, one of the machines broke down, in the midst of producing a large export order for an important new overseas customer. George allocated Steve Johnson and Dave Hopkins to fix the machine urgently. At the end of the day Mike found out from George that Steve and Dave had gone home at 5 p.m., leaving the machine half repaired, in spite of George having asked them to work on and finish it. When Mike insisted that he wanted the machine repaired straight away, otherwise the important export order would not be ready for shipment on the agreed date, George told him that Steve and Dave were not prepared to work overtime because of the company's new 'overtime ban'.

At this point, Mike decided he ought to inform Andrew Whittaker of the problem. When Andrew heard what had happened, he asked to see everyone concerned, first thing the next morning, in his office.

THE BRIEF

In groups of five, you will be asked to role play the situation in Andrew Whittaker's office the next day. When you have decided which role you are going to play and have read all the descriptions below of the characters, you will need to act out your role, bringing out your side of the story, in relation to the other people involved. The group's eventual aim is to resolve the dispute.

ROLE DESCRIPTIONS

ANDREW WHITTAKER, MANAGING DIRECTOR

Age 54, married with two children. Bought the company 15 years ago, when it was struggling, with the redundancy money from his previous job as marketing manager with a well-known company. Highly respected by the workers, though they see less of him nowadays as the company has expanded.

MIKE HUTCHINGS, PRODUCTION MANAGER

Age 39, unmarried. Loyal, works long hours and is ambitious. Aims to be a director of the firm one day and is keen to show he has a firm grip of things. Has worked his way up from the shop floor.

GEORGE COLLINS, MAINTENANCE SUPERVISOR

Age 56, married with three children. Has been with the firm since it started. Was a supervisor when Mike started as a trainee with the firm. A steady, reliable employee. Prefers the way things were done in the old days and is looking forward to his retirement.

STEVE JOHNSON

Age 34, married. Been with the firm two and a half years. Good at his job but does not go looking for extra work. A bit of a loner, he never goes out with the other lads on Fridays for a drink after work. Can get 'in a huff' at times.

DAVE HOPKINS

Age 28, married with two young children. Has been with the firm 12 years, since he joined as an apprentice at 16. He likes it there and is a good worker. Enjoys going out with the other lads on Friday nights and gets on well with everyone.

Discussion points

1 Why might Andrew Whittaker have been concerned about overtime levels?

2 How far can the dispute be said to have arisen through poor communications in the organisation:
   a) downwards from the management to the shop floor?
   b) upwards from the shop floor to the management?

3 Why is there a need for different communication channels in the firm now, compared to when it was a small firm?

4 To what extent might the situation have been aggravated by possible personality clashes between the people involved?

5 Taking each person in turn, describe how far you think he was responsible for the dispute which arose.

6 How was the dispute eventually resolved in each of your groups?

7 What might have happened if the dispute had not ended at this stage?

8 How might the presence of a trade union have:
   a) helped
   b) hindered
   the resolution of this dispute?

9 In what ways is this situation:
   a) typical
   b) untypical
   of the way disputes can happen?

Finance

IN ASSOCIATION WITH  Lloyds Bank

Introduction: what is the role of finance?

All businesses need to make a profit in order to survive. The most successful firms are those that never lose sight of this basic fact and that carefully assess the profitability of any step they take. The role of the finance department is crucial in this respect. It involves not only keeping track of all the firm's transactions but also advising on the amounts which should be raised for particular purposes and the most appropriate sources of finance. The finance department also operates systems for maintaining tight controls on spending and analyses the firm's financial performance from the accounts produced.

Firms need to raise enough capital for their **fixed assets**, such as land, buildings and machinery, and also to provide enough **working capital** for their day-to-day needs, such as wages, raw materials and so on. Costs need to be known in order to plan budgets, calculate prices and work out profit levels. Most importantly, the **break-even point** at which **costs** equal **sales revenue** needs to be established, as it is only sales above this point which produce a profit. The break-even point can determine whether it is worth accepting a particular order. It can also determine whether a product should be made any longer. Firms can adopt various strategies to improve their profitability such as raising prices, cutting costs, increasing sales or improving the product/customer mix.

The company's objectives largely determine how much capital is raised and what proportion of this is **equity capital** (from owners' capital or shareholders' funds) or **loan capital** (from bank loans, hire purchases etc.). There are dangers in borrowing too much, leading to a high **gearing ratio**, where the profits generated by the business are not enough to meet repayments on the loans. Borrowing too little and being **undercapitalised** can be as dangerous because the firm cannot then operate efficiently.

Keeping track of the money involves setting up a **book-keeping system** to record day-to-day transactions – flows of money which come in from customers and which go out as payments on bills. The information from these books or **ledgers** is then extracted and summarised into company accounts. The two main accounts are the **profit and loss account**, which provides a history of the company's trading, and the **balance sheet**, which acts like a snapshot of the company's financial position at a particular moment in time. Aided by the use of computers, companies are producing these accounts far more regularly, not just at the end of the financial year when they have to be **audited** and checked for inaccuracies. Monthly and weekly reporting is now quite common. The company's financial performance can then be interpreted from the accounts using a variety of **ratios**.

Most firms also carry out regular **cash flow forecasts**, to predict their requirements for cash so they can ensure that they have enough money to be able to pay their bills as they fall due. This is essential, as even highly profitable businesses can go under if they run into cash flow problems.

Well-run firms generally put part of their profits back into the business as an **investment** for the future.

How are costs worked out?

Firms need to work out their costs in order to plan budgets and calculate the profits they expect to make. The costs they incur are of three main types:

- **Fixed costs** These remain fairly static in the short term and *do not* immediately change with the volume of output. Fixed costs include council tax, rent, machinery, insurance and so on, which still have to be paid however little is produced. This is why it is uneconomic for factories to operate at **production capacity** levels which do not cover their fixed costs.

  Indirect costs or general **overheads** are not associated with the production of any particular product and are normally fixed costs. Such costs are essential for the general administration of the business. They include the cost of **indirect labour**, such as typists, accountants, managers, sales staff etc., and **indirect materials**, such as advertising leaflets, all of which cannot be attributed to a specific product.

- **Variable costs** These *do* change with the volume of output. Variable costs include mainly the cost of labour and raw materials, but electricity, overtime payments and maintenance costs also fluctuate according to how much is produced, falling when output decreases and rising when it increases.

- **Semi-variable costs** These are partly fixed and partly variable. For instance, the rental cost of a photocopier is a fixed cost, but the cost of paper is a variable cost, as it depends on how much is used.

METHODS OF COSTING

Having classified their costs into different types, the next step for firms is to decide how to cost the products they make.

- **Absorption costing** This is based on the principle that all costs incurred by a business should be absorbed by production. When a business produces a single product, it is fairly easy to charge all costs to that product. However, when many products are made, it becomes more difficult to allocate costs accurately between products, especially general overheads. How much of the cost of a salesperson's salary or of a telephone bill should be allocated to a particular product?

- **Marginal or contribution costing** This is based on the principle that fixed costs need to be paid whatever the level of output. Once the variable costs of producing a product have been taken away from its **revenue** or selling price, the amount left makes a **contribution** to the fixed costs of production.

ACTIVITY

Quik Kalc Ltd: analysing break-even points

You work in the financial department of Quik Kalc Ltd, a rapidly expanding firm which manufactures calculators, aimed at the 'volume' end of the market. Mr Singh, the senior accountant, has asked you to work out the exact level of output at which the firm breaks even or just recovers its costs. Quik Kalc's fixed costs are £4,000. Each calculator costs £2 to make in terms of variable costs (labour and materials) and sells for £3. In order to work out the **break-even point**, you will need to use these figures when you fill in your copy of the table on the next page to show the costs and revenue at different output levels.

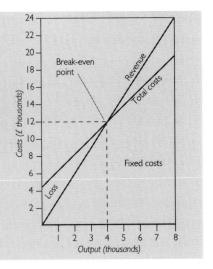

Output	Fixed costs	Variable costs (Multiply by output level)	Total costs (Add fixed and variable costs)	Revenue (Multiply price by output)
0	4,000	0	4,000	0
1,000	4,000	2,000	6,000	3,000
2,000				
3,000				
4,000				
5,000				
6,000				
7,000				
8,000				

The results from the table you have filled in have been plotted on the previous page. You will see that the break-even point occurs when Quik Kalc produces 4,000 calculators. This can also be worked out by a simple calculation. One of their calculators costs £2 to make in terms of variable costs and sells for £3, so each calculator sold makes a contribution of £1 towards fixed costs. As the fixed costs are £4,000, this means 4,000 calculators have to be sold before the break-even point is reached. If Quik Kalc sells any more than 4,000 it makes a profit and if it sells any fewer it makes a loss. The greater the output, the greater the profit, though eventually a stage will be reached when the fixed costs will have to rise to cater for the increased production.

ACTIVITY

Analysing the factors effecting break-even points

Use the simple calculation method described above to work out the new break-even point (if any) in the following situations. (Figures remain the same unless otherwise stated.)

1 Quik Kalc begins to experience fierce competition and has to reduce the selling price of each calculator to £2.50.
2 Demand increases in the months before Christmas and Quik Kalc raises the selling price of £4 per calculator.
3 A shortage of raw materials encourages suppliers to put up their prices by £1 so the variable costs are now £3 per calculator.
4 A severe recession forces Quik Kalc to reduce the selling price to £2.
5 The selling price remains at £2 during the recession, but efficiency savings reduce fixed costs to £1,000.
6 Explain why the break-even point changed in questions 1 and 2.
7 Why was it not possible to break even in questions 3 and 4?
8 Why was it not possible to break even in question 5 in spite of fixed costs being reduced drastically?

Profit is not a dirty word

One of the most obvious ways in which firms can increase their profits is by **raising prices**. This can be fairly easily done in times of inflation, but even then it is a strategy that will only work if the market accepts the new prices. If not, sales decrease, defeating the object of the exercise.

Another alternative is to **cut fixed and variable costs**. A classic example of the impact of this strategy is provided by British Leyland (BL). Without government help, BL would have gone out of business long ago. In 1975 alone it made a net loss of £123.5 million. The unenviable task of making BL profitable again faced Michael Edwardes when he became chairman in 1977. One of the most important aspects of his recovery strategy was to cut costs. During his time ten major plants were closed, the workforce was more than halved and strict cost controls were introduced, especially in purchasing – a particularly important area in view of the fact that raw materials and components account for 60 per cent of the cost of a car. These measures reduced costs by at least £250 million a year compared to 1978 levels.

Cost savings can also be achieved by cutting administrative overheads. In fact, getting rid of a large central headquarters building with its office staff has been the first step in many successful turnarounds, transforming companies from ailing loss makers to profitable concerns. When Arunbhai Patel bought the Finlays newsagent chain from Hanson Trust in 1987, he turned a £1.5 million loss into a handsome profit almost overnight, largely by the closure of the head office.

Companies can also improve profit by **increasing sales**, though to achieve this might mean lowering prices or having to increase fixed and variable costs to cope with the extra production. Instead of selling more, some may therefore choose instead to concentrate on the best selling product lines or those where profit margins are highest, and thus **improve the product mix**. To **improve the customer mix** by concentrating on supplying the right customers can also prove highly profitable.

In recent years some firms have chosen to improve their profitability by **reducing investment**. Certainly, if little or no money is spent on research and development or on new technology, the impact is to reduce spending and show improved profits in the short term, without any immediately disastrous effects. But what of the future? Inevitably the price of such a short-sighted policy is stagnation and eventual decline, as the company loses market share to competitors who *have* made long-term investments in these crucial areas.

Discussion point

What are the dangers of firms seeking to increase profits at any cost?

Profit and loss accounts

Profit and loss accounts (P and L accounts) provide a 'history' of the company's finances during the previous year for a particular period. They are made up of three sections:

- **Trading section** This shows the **revenue** from sales and the **costs** incurred in producing those sales (that is, the cost of materials and labour). The cost of sales taken away from the sales revenue gives the **gross profit**.
- **Profit or loss section** This shows the costs of general overheads such as administration and distribution. The cost of **depreciation** of fixed assets is also included. (Depreciation is the amount by which an item loses value because of its age and any wear and tear.) This total is deducted from gross profit to give the **operating profit**. Any interest payments are deducted from operating profit to give the **net profit before tax**.

- **Appropriation section** This shows how the profit left is set aside or appropriated – that is, how much is distributed to shareholders and how much remains as **retained profits** or reserves.

Balance sheets

A balance sheet provides a 'snapshot' of the company's wealth at a particular moment in time. It is made up of three sections:

- **Assets**
  a) **Fixed assets** are assets which are not regularly sold by the business. They include **tangible assets** such as land, factories and machines, and **intangible assets** which are less concrete but nevertheless do have a value, such as spending on research and development.
  b) **Current assets** are assets which are expected to be converted into cash within the next 12 months. They range, according to their ease of being turned into cash, from stocks, debtors and shares in subsidiary companies to actual cash, which is the most **liquid** asset of all.
- **Creditors**
  a) **Current liabilities** are debts where repayment is due within the year, such as overdrafts or goods bought on credit. When current liabilities are taken away from current assets, this gives **net current assets**. If the value of fixed assets is then added to this, it gives the value of **total assets (less current liabilities)**.
  b) **Long-term liabilities** are debts on which repayment is due after a year – for instance, on long-term bank loans. When this figure is subtracted from total assets, it gives the final value of **net assets**.
- **Capital and reserves** The company's **issued share capital**, which is the value of shares (based on their **nominal value** when issued, not on their current market price), is added to the company's reserves or retained profit. This total figure *must* balance with the net assets figure.

FIXED ASSETS	£	£
Intangible assets	-	
Tangible assets	468,000	
Investments	64,000	532,000
CURRENT ASSETS		
Stocks	78,500	
Debtors	61,800	
Investments	-	
Cash at bank and in hand	8,750	
		149,050
CREDITORS (Amounts falling due within one year)		
Bank loans and overdraft	59,300	
Other creditors	16,700	
Corporation tax	23,000	
TOTAL CURRENT LIABILITIES		99.000
NET CURRENT ASSETS		50,050
TOTAL ASSETS LESS CURRENT LIABILITIES		582,050
CREDITORS (Amounts falling due after one year)		
Bank loans	40,000	
Other creditors	-	
		40,000
NET ASSETS		542,050
CAPITAL AND RESERVES		
Share capital	100,000	
Profit and loss account		
(reserves)	442,050	
		542,050

Balance sheet

	£	£
TURNOVER		112,199
COST OF SALES		
Raw materials	32,110	
Labour	24,432	
Fuel and power	6,732	
TOTAL COST OF SALES		63,274
GROSS PROFIT		48,925
COST OF OVERHEADS		
Staff salaries	14,989	
Administration and		
distribution	4,722	
Rates, rent and insurance	9,955	
Depreciation	3,250	
TOTAL COST OF OVERHEADS		32,916
OPERATING PROFIT		16,009
Interest payable		2,385
NET PROFIT BEFORE TAX		13,624
Tax		3,130
NET PROFIT AFTER TAX		10,494
Dividend to Shareholders		
RETAINED PROFIT TRANSFERRED		
TO RESERVES		10,494

Profit and loss account

ACTIVITY

Preparing a P and L account

Using the example given above, prepare a P and L account for Grant Morgan Ltd from the following information.

Last year, Grant Morgan Ltd sold bicycles worth a total of £750,000. The company paid £70,000 in wages for its shop-floor employees and £35,000 for its managers, sales staff and office staff. A further £475,000 went on steel and components, £6,000 was spent on photocopying, office stationery etc. and £8,600 on insurance cover. During the year the interest paid on loans came to £5,800, and £40,000 was spent on power to manufacture the bicycles. The company estimated that the depreciation cost of the machinery was £8,000. The tax bill for the year amounted to £22,300.

Directors of Grant Morgan have decided that 30 per cent of the remaining profit will be distributed to shareholders and that 70 per cent will be retained as reserves.

ACTIVITY

Preparing a balance sheet

Using the example given above, prepare a balance sheet for Image Scan Ltd from the following information.

Image Scan Ltd was formed with a share capital of £60,000. The company bought a factory and office for £80,000 and spent £13,500 on equipment in order to make its range of photocopiers. To finance this, they borrowed £40,000 on a term loan from the bank, of which £4,000 is repayable within the year. The warehouse has stocks of £38,000, for which £18,000 has already been paid to suppliers, leaving the remaining amount outstanding on trade credit. Customers owe £23,000 in unpaid bills. During the period Image Scan Ltd have been operating, they have managed to retain £27,500 of their profits for reinvestment, after having allowed £7,000 in corporation tax.

Where do firms raise finance?

The source of finance which is best in a particular situation depends on:

- **the firm's financial position.** When a firm has borrowed as much as it can, yet still cannot meet its commitments because of slow-paying customers, it may turn to **debt factoring** (see Table 6.1). Those who wish to spread the cost of equipment they cannot afford to buy outright may consider bank loans, hire purchase or leasing. Firms who meet the stringent financial requirements of the Stock Exchange may raise finance by selling shares. Most firms have an overdraft facility so they can borrow varying amounts for short periods of time, which gives them the flexibility to cope with temporary demands for cash. Many also take advantage of the trade credit offered by suppliers to improve their cash flow.
- **the firm's financial objectives.** When a firm's owners are concerned with survival, they will tend to adopt a policy of raising capital by using their own savings or reinvesting any profits rather than borrowing, in order to avoid diluting financial control. On the other hand, firms that are concerned with expansion will be prepared to consider raising finance by issuing stocks and shares, seeking venture capital or obtaining mortgage loans.

Table 6.1 *Types of short-term finance (under 2 years)*

Source of finance	Advantages	Disadvantages
Bank overdraft	Simple to arrange. Flexible, as amounts borrowed can vary up to the limit arranged. Relatively cheap, as interest is charged only on the actual amount borrowed, for the number of days overdrawn.	Interest charged is between 2.5 per cent and 4 per cent over bank base lending rate, so can work out expensive over long periods. If limit is exceeded the overdraft facility can be withdrawn and immediate repayment demanded.
Trade credit	Improves the flow of money as suppliers often give as long as three months to pay invoices. A free form of credit.	The prompt payment discount which many firms offer is lost if the trade credit is used. The benefits are reduced by firms having to offer their customers time to pay. If payment is made after the credit period, suppliers may refuse to send goods in future, or may insist on cash in advance.
Debt factoring	Capital tied up in money owed by customers is released. The factoring company takes over the debt and advances up to 80 per cent of the amount owed straight away. This improves the firm's cash flow. The factoring company then sends out invoices and chases up the debtor, paying the remainder of the debt to the firm when the customer settles up – less their charge.	Factoring companies can charge as much as 5 per cent of the bill for their service. They tend only to be interested in handling bills from firms with large turnovers.

Short-term finance can be used to:

- Bridge the 'finance gap' as working capital fluctuates between customers paying late and raw materials having to be paid for in advance.
- Provide working capital where there are seasonal variations in sales patterns.
- Finance the purchase of assets with a short life cycle.
- Cover temporary needs for extra funds due to unexpected problems.

Table 6.2 *Types of medium-term finance (2–5 years)*

Source of finance	Advantages	Disadvantages
Bank term loan	Financial planning is made easier as repayments are made in regular instalments. Relatively simple to arrange once the bank's lending criteria have been met.	Interest rates charged on loans vary, with small businesses generally paying higher rates as they are seen as presenting a higher risk. Fixed rates can prove dangerous if interest rates drop after the rate was fixed. For this reason, most businesses prefer variable interest rates.
Leasing	When vehicles and equipment are leased or rented from a leasing company, the firm is able to use equipment which it could not otherwise afford to buy outright. Working capital can then be used for other purposes. Some leasing agreements include the carrying out of maintenance. Leased equipment can be changed when it becomes obsolete, unlike purchased equipment which has to be kept for longer to recover the the initial investment.	The vehicles and equipment which are leased are not owned by the firm. The rental charges add up over a period of time, to the point where the firm has effectively paid for the goods even though the goods cannot be classed as company assets, because they are still owned by the company renting them out.
Hire purchase	After an initial down-payment for the vehicle or equipment, goods are purchased in instalments over a period of 2 years. This means the cost is spread and is more manageable than an up-front payment for outright purchase. Unlike leased goods those bought on hire purchase are owned after the last repayment is made.	Goods remain the property of the finance house until full repayment has been made, so if any payments are missed the finance house can repossess the goods. A more expensive form of borrowing than bank loans.

Medium-term finance can be used to:

- Finance the purchase of assets such as plant and equipment which have a longer life.
- Provide initial start-up capital to invest in fixed assets.
- Replace an overdraft which is difficult to clear.

Table 6.3 *Types of long-term finance (over 5 years)*

Source of finance	Advantages	Disadvantages
Owners' savings (in the case of a sole trader or partnership)	Owners use their own capital (from a second mortgage, life insurance policy, savings etc.) to inject capital into the business, which reduces the amount borrowed on which interest has to be paid. Owners retain more control than if financial control is diluted by the sale of shares.	Owners' capital is tied up and cannot easily be taken out of business. Owners' capital is at risk if business fails – they are liable to lose their own home and other possessions.
Sale of shares (in the case of a private limited company or plublic limited company)	The main advantage of issuing shares is that the shareholders have **limited liability** if the business fails. Personal possessions are not at risk and their liability is limited to the actual capital invested. Capital is raised by issuing **shares** (which are a proportion of what the company is worth) to investors, who are encouraged to buy by the promise of receiving **dividends** or profits on their shares. Shares can be sold as **preference shares** which offer a fixed **return** and have priority when dividens are paid over ordinary shareholders. **Ordinary shares** offer a variable return as profits change from year to year, according to how well the company has done.	The administrative cost of issuing shares is high. It is difficult to estimate the market price of shares, though this problem can be avoided if they are issued by **tender**, where investors state how much they are willing to pay for them. The price of shares can go up or down and shareholders may have to sell at a lower price than they bought at. A listing or **quotation** on the Stock Exchange is needed so a company's shares can be bought or sold on the exchange. This is difficult to obtain as financial requirements are stringent in order to safeguard the interests of people buying and selling shares.
Reinvested profits	Capital can be raised by the company reinvesting or ploughing back the profits made at the end of the year, after expenses and dividends to shareholders have been paid.	Profits may be scarce or non-existent, especially in times of recession. Expansion may be slow and limited for companies relying on self-financed growth.
Mortgage loans	Capital is often supplied by pension or insurance funds for a loan over 25–30 years for buildings or land, with the asset as security.	The loans are usually only given when large sums are required.
Venture capital loans	Capital is supplied by venture capital firms who accept a certain degree of risk as being inevitable. Most venture capitalists also provide help in the form of back-up management and financial expertise. The government's **business expansion scheme** offers incentives to private investors willing to invest in unquoted companies.	Most venture capitalists are only interested in loans for more than £50,000 and some only consider ventures where more than £250,000 is involved, as the administration costs are not worthwhile on smaller projects. They charge a negotiation fee for arranging the finance. They generally expect a non-controlling **equity stake** of 20–40 per cent in the firm's capital, as a return for their investment.
Government loans	Capital can be raised for eligible companies from local authorities, government enterprise agencies and regional selective assistance. Capital can also be raised from the EEC.	The vetting procedures needed to minimise risk can cause long delays in obtaining the grants.
Debenture loans	Individuals can supply capital to a company in the form of long-term loans called **debentures** which have to be repaid on an agreed date. These repayments take priority over payments to all other shareholders.	Generally the company has to offer some security for the loan, which can be sold if the company cannot meet the repayments. In the case of a **fixed debenture** this is a specific asset such as a building, and in the case of a **floating debenture** it can be any asset owned by the company.

Long-term finance can be used to:

- Finance the purchase of assets with a longer life, such as buildings.
- Provide expansion capital for major purchases such as the acquisition of other companies or the purchase of a new factory.

ACTIVITY

Choosing the most appropriate source of finance

For each of the following descriptions, state which source of finance you think it is most appropriate to use. Explain your decision in each case.

1. A firm that wishes to finance a major purchase of land for a new factory.
2. A successful firm where the owners are willing to dilute financial control in order to expand, by giving up part of their equity.
3. A firm that has borrowed as much as it can but cannot pay its expenses until slow-paying customers pay their bills.
4. A firm that has to decide between paying a bill from British Telecom or a bill from a supplier, both of which were received two weeks ago.
5. An established firm, quoted on the Stock Exchange, which wishes to raise money from the public to be repaid after a specific period of time.
6. A firm that wishes to spread the cost of high capital outlay on equipment and has borrowed the maximum possible from the bank.
7. A firm which will create many new jobs and is being set up in a depressed area.
8. A successful, well-run, private limited company which has expanded as far as possible on self-financed growth.
9. A firm that has bills from suppliers which are due for payment now, though money owed by customers will not come in for a few weeks.
10. A small firm started by an entrepreneur who intends to trade on a small scale initially and who wishes to retain full control of the business.
11. A firm whose owners intend to expand at a steady rate without diluting financial control and without borrowing too much.
12. A firm in a high-technology industry which does not wish to purchase all the expensive equipment it needs.
13. A firm that wishes to raise finance to invest in buildings and equipment.

Do profits equal cash?

How can a highly profitable firm go out of business? Unfortunately, if cash flow is not managed properly this can happen all too easily. No matter how great the profits, a firm that becomes **insolvent** and cannot pay its debts may go out of business if all its **creditors** decide to call in the money owed to them. Early warning signs which might appear long before this stage is reached include finding difficulty in raising finance and obtaining credit, having to borrow at uneconomic rates and not being able to operate efficiently – for instance, not having the funds to buy in bulk.

It is the *timing* of flows of cash into and out of the firm which is crucial, not the total amount of cash generated. This is aptly summed up by one company chairman who has built a thriving business in the space of a few short years. 'Companies don't go bust because they lose money, they go bust because they run out of money. If you stay cash-rich, you stand a much greater chance of success. Maybe not as big a success, but a more secure success.'

METHODS OF IMPROVING CASH FLOW

- **Raising extra capital** – reinvesting profits, taking out loans, using owners' capital (in the case of sole traders and partnerships) or issuing shares (in the case of limited companies).
- **Reducing the cash operating cycle** – shortening the time between purchase of raw materials and sale of finished goods, so that cash is not tied up for too long.
- **Sale and lease back** – selling fixed assets to a leasing company to raise money and then leasing them back.
- **Reducing investment** – reducing the amount spent on fixed assets such as new machines or new factories.
- **Delaying payment** – taking longer to pay bills and using trade credit.
- **Spreading purchase costs** – using bank loans, hire purchase or leasing to spread the cost of payment in instalments.
- **Tight stock control** – ensuring capital is not tied up in too much stock.

- **Tight credit control** – making sure that debtors pay their bills by prompt invoicing and reminders; checking customers' credit-worthiness before goods are sent out.
- **Debt factoring** – selling debts to a factoring company to raise cash immediately.

Discussion point

Is there a problem-free way of improving cash flow?

Having improved their cash flow and maintained **liquidity** so that they can pay bills as they fall due, firms also need to carry out regular **cash flow forecasts** in order to predict the flow of money over a period of time. The importance of this is shown in the next activity.

FINAL ACTIVITY

The sixth-form disco

BACKGROUND

As part of the school's fund-raising drive for a new minibus, the sixth form have decided to hold a monthly disco during the autumn and spring terms. The head is prepared to put in £200 to get the scheme off the ground, but has made it clear that no more funds will be made available after this. You will therefore need to carry out a cash flow forecast to make sure that you do not run out of cash in any particular month.

THE BRIEF

The regular expenses incurred for each disco are listed in the cash flow forecast table. You have also agreed to repay the head's loan at the rate of £50 per month. The money coming in will be from the sale of refreshments, where you will expect to make a 100 per cent profit on what you buy. The suppliers will allow you seven days' credit. You will also be charging an entrance free of £1 a head and expect eighty people to turn up each month.

Use these figures and the example for October to plan your forecast for November. To find the closing balance at the end of a month, add the opening balance to the total receipts and take the total payments away from this. Then carry this closing balance figure forward as the opening balance for the next month.

Then plan the cash flow forecasts for the remaining months after November. You need to take into account the special circumstances listed below:

- **In December** You intend to hold a special Christmas disco. It is likely that 150 people will turn up and the extra refreshments will cost £200. You plan to spend £40 on sundries such as Christmas decorations.
- **In January** The DJ has told you that he intends to increase his fee to £100 in the New Year. You want to buy a set of lights from a local electrical store, which will be reduced to £45 in the sales.
- **In February** Many sixth-formers will be away on the school skiing trip. You expect fifty people to turn up so you only need to spend £70 on refreshments.
- **In March** You plan to sell the lights, which are no longer needed, and expect to get £30 for them.

On your copy of the table, write in the forecast for each month.

1 What would have happened if your suppliers of refreshments had not given you seven days' credit?
2 When did you make the last repayment to the head?
3 How much were you able to contribute to the minibus fund at the end of the six discos?

Cash flow forecast for sixth form disco

	Oct	Nov	Dec	Jan	Feb	Mar
Opening balance (brought forward)	200					
Recepits:	(loan)					
Door takings	80					
Sale of refreshments	200					
Other receipts	0					
Total receipts	280					
Payments:						
Disco hire and DJ	70					
Hire of lights	20					
Advertising posyters/leaflets	10					
Purchase of refreshments	100					
Sundry expenses	10					
Repayments to head	50					
Other repayments	0					
Total payments	260					
Closing balance (carried forward)	220					

Management

IN ASSOCIATION WITH ALLIED‡LYONS

Introduction: doing the right things

A good definition of a manager is 'An individual who is accountable for more work than he/she can do themselves and who gets some of it done through other people' (W Brown and E Jacques). This definition includes managers who function at all levels, from operational manager right up to the chief executive at the top of the organisation. The **span of control**, however, or number of employees whose work is directed by managers at different levels, will obviously vary.

Successful managers have invariably learnt the difference between efficiency and effectiveness. Managers who have the ability to 'do things right' will merely be efficient, but to be really effective a manager must 'do the right things' – in other words, produce results. Peter Drucker, in his book *The Effective Executive*, describes five practices which are necessary for effectiveness.

Effective executives:

- **Know where their time goes.** 'They systematically manage the small amount of their time that they can control.'
- **Focus on outward contribution.** 'They start with the question "What results are expected of me?", rather than starting with what work needs to be done.'
- **Build on strengths.** This includes building on 'their own strengths, the strengths of their superiors, colleagues and subordinates and on the strengths in the situation – that is, on what they *can* do.'
- **Concentrate on a few major areas.** 'They force themselves to set priorities.'
- **Make effective decisions.** 'They make judgements after taking into account a variety of opposing viewpoints. The decisions they make are few but fundamental.'

What does a manager do?

The earliest attempt at isolating what a manager's job involves was made by Henri Fayol, whose writings were first published in English in 1947. Based on his own management experience in the French mining industry, he arrived at a definition of the role of a manager – which was to:

- **Forecast and plan** – examining the future and drawing up a plan of action.
- **Organise** – building up the organisation's structure so that plans can be carried out effectively.
- **Command** – obtaining the best possible performance from the personnel.
- **Co-ordinate** – making sure each department's efforts harmonise with other departments.
- **Control** – making sure everything works according to plan.

Later on, in 1973, Henry Mintzberg's approach was more concerned with what managers *actually* do, as opposed to what they ought to do. On the basis of studies of managers' work activity, he showed in *The Nature of Managerial Work* that managers perform a wide variety of roles.

These 10 roles can be grouped into three broad areas:

- **Interpersonal** – the relationships a manager has to have with others.
- **Informational** – the collecting and passing on of information.
- **Decisional** – the making of different kinds of decisions.

Of course, Mintzberg recognised that these roles can be combined in a number of different ways according to the manager's own personality, the situation he or she is in, the kind of job he or she does and the general environment.

ACTIVITY

Classification of a manager's roles

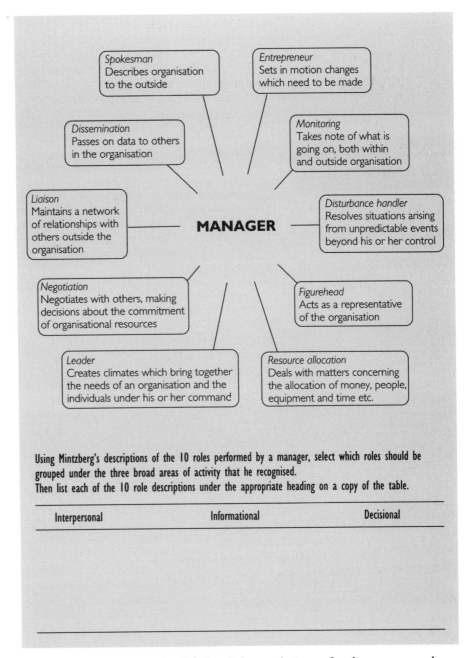

Spokesman
Describes organisation to the outside

Entrepreneur
Sets in motion changes which need to be made

Dissemination
Passes on data to others in the organisation

Monitoring
Takes note of what is going on, both within and outside organisation

Liaison
Maintains a network of relationships with others outside the organisation

MANAGER

Disturbance handler
Resolves situations arising from unpredictable events beyond his or her control

Negotiation
Negotiates with others, making decisions about the commitment of organisational resources

Figurehead
Acts as a representative of the organisation

Leader
Creates climates which bring together the needs of an organisation and the individuals under his or her command

Resource allocation
Deals with matters concerning the allocation of money, people, equipment and time etc.

Using Mintzberg's descriptions of the 10 roles performed by a manager, select which roles should be grouped under the three broad areas of activity that he recognised.
Then list each of the 10 role descriptions under the appropriate heading on a copy of the table.

Interpersonal	Informational	Decisional

Discussion points

1 How many of these roles does your headteacher probably carry out?

2 Are some roles more important than others?

What qualities do managers need?

In 1988, a report called 'What Makes a Manager?' was published by the Institute of Manpower Studies (IMS), which looked at how 40 leading UK employers defined managerial skills. The report, reviewed by Michael Syrett in *Director* magazine, found that the qualities these employers looked for most often were the ability to communicate, leadership, judgement, initiative, organisational skills and motivation. Other attributes less frequently mentioned by employers, but still regarded as important, were planning, innovation, good appearance, interpersonal skills, maturity and numeracy.

One of the co-authors of the report, Wendy Hirsh, says that, 'The need for managers to deal with change was apparent in the frequent mention of adaptability, the capacity to deal with stress and the need for personal energy.' She added that, 'Employers also tend to look for "macho" managers with rather assertive personalities. Where sensitivity is needed, it tends to be expressed in terms of skills, for example the ability to work in teams, rather than in personality.'

In the next activity, you will be asked within groups of five to rank these management qualities yourselves and decide which *you* think are most important.

ACTIVITY

Ranking of management attributes

On your individual copy of the table below, rank each management attribute in order of importance from 1 to 16 and write the ranking in your column. Rank the attribute you rate as being most important as 1, through to the least important as 16. Collect the rankings of other members in your group onto your table. Add the figures across and fill in the column for the group's total ranking. the **lowest** total (nearest to 5) is the most important attribute, the next lowest the second most important attribute, and so on. What do your results reveal?

Management qualities identified by IMS report	Group member 1	Group member 2	Group member 3	Group member 4	Group member 5	Group's total ranking for each quality	Final order of importance for each quality
Communication							
Leadership							
Judgement							
Initiative							
Organisational skills							
Motivation							
Planning							
Innovation							
Good appearance							
Interpersonal skills							
Maturity							
Numeracy							
Adaptability							
Stress handling							
Personal energy							
Assertiveness							

1   a) Did you generally agree or disagree as a group?
    b) Were there any attributes you all agreed or disagreed on?
2   Was anyone's ranking vastly different to the others?
3   Are there any attributes that you think are important which are not on the list?

Discussion point

Why would the attributes which are regarded as important vary from company to company?

Is there a typical manager?

Your answers to the activity ranking managers' qualities probably showed some agreement within your group about the most important qualities needed by managers. Does this mean, then, that there is a type of person who is a 'typical' manager?

The need for management to become a chartered profession was clearly stated by John Banham when he was CBI chief, at an annual conference of the Institute of Personnel Management. 'There is a misguided belief that management is nothing but applied common sense and the realm of the gifted amateur', he said, adding that, 'If we want to attract the most talented people into our business, management must become a profession with its own qualifications.' In other words, we need to have chartered managers as we have chartered accountants and chartered surveyors.

The concept of a chartered manager does, however, presume the existence of a universally accepted set of skills and knowledge. Certainly, the IMS report showed a great degree of consensus among the UK companies surveyed as to the qualities they looked for in managers. However, as Wendy Hirsh points out, the same terms can vary in meaning according to the company culture and job role of the manager. 'Good decision making in one company means taking innovative decisions, in another it means analysing hard data and minimising commercial risk.' The implication, therefore, is that skills gained in one company, which are closely related to the way things are done there, are not easily transferable to another company which is run on very different lines.

In any case, as John Kotter of Harvard Business School points out in his book *The Leadership Factor*, 'Figuring out the right thing to do in an environment of uncertainty caused by intense competitive activity and then getting others, often many others, to accept a new way of doing things demands skills and approaches that most managers simply did not need in the relatively calm 1950s, 1960s and early 1970s. It demands something more than technical expertise, administrative ability and traditional (especially bureaucratic) management. Operating in the new environment also requires leadership.'

What do Britain's top executives earn?

Table 7.1 *Executives' salaries over £500,000*

Company	Chairman or Chief Executive	Highest Paid Director
Glaxo Holdings	Sir Paul Girolami	£1,440,000
Hanson	Derek Bonham	£1,360,000
Tomkins	Greg Hutchings	£1,235,000
SmithKline Beecham	Robert Bauman	£1,015,000
Tesco	Sir Ian Maclaurin	£967,000
Cable and Wireless	Lord Young	£863,410
BOC	Patrick Rich	£786,393
Guinness	Sir Anthony Tennant	£777,000
Marks and Spencer (UK)	Sir Richard Greenbury	£721,126
Unilever	Sir Michael Perry	£695,102
British Airways	Sir Colin Marshall	£665,000
Boots	Sir James Blyth	£620,000
Bass	Ian Prosser	£615,000
Ladbroke	John Jackson	£585,000
British Telecom	Sir Iain Vallance	£560,000
British Petroleum	David Simon	£530,000
Carlton Communications	Michael Green	£530,000
ICI	Sir Denys Henderson	£526,000
Vodafone Group	Gerry Whent	£515,144
GEC	Lord Weinstock	£514,000

Source: 'How much do other people earn?' by Eleanor Mills, *The Observer*, 16 January, 1994
Note: The top director's salary is not necessarily that of the chairman or chief executive. All figures are from the most recently published annual report of each company. Highest Paid Directors' salaries exclude pension payments and share options.

Discussion points

1 Can any person's abilities be worth over £415,000 a year?

2 What impact can a good top executive have on a firm's fortunes?

3 Are high salaries needed to attract and keep top executives?

4 What other benefits might top executives get?

What makes a leader?

Ask anyone to explain what makes a leader and they would probably describe figures like Napoleon, Churchill, Golda Meir, Mahatma Gandhi or Martin Luther King – leaders who had such personal charisma they drew people to them like magnets and whose supporters wholeheartedly gave of their time, effort and commitment in following their leaders' goals. Famous examples such as these, which influence popular conceptions of what leaders are like, encourage most people to think that they could never aspire to being leaders.

Yet most definitions view the essence of leadership as being the ability to motivate groups to achieve certain goals, without the use of any force or coercion. On this basis, many more people can be seen to function as leaders, though not perhaps with the same verve and dash as the truly inspirational figures. In fact, as firms today fight for survival in intensely competitive world markets, the need for leaders at all levels, not just at executive level, has never been greater.

Michael Edwardes, the former chairman of BL, is quoted in Berry Ritchie and Walter Goldsmith's *The New Elite* describing the qualities he thinks good leaders have in common. 'They have this driving force inside them and people follow them because they inspire trust. They create confidence that they know what they are doing. The good leader is someone who is followed, rather than someone who obviously leads. People make the leader.'

Clearly leaders' influence stems from their acceptance by the group, and though this influence may often be reinforced by the power and authority conferred by their position within the organisation, acceptance is nevertheless not dependent on their formal status. In fact, any leaders who try and rely on their rank to command authority will never have more than a tenuous hold on their group. Respect must be earned, as it will not be automatically accorded by virtue of a person's job title or rank. Groups may reject a leader they do not respect, and if this happens they are likely to do the minimum required and may even work towards sabotaging the leader's efforts. Strong leadership is therefore essential if groups are to work productively.

In an interview with George Bickerstaffe of *Director* magazine, John Adair, the UK's leading authority on the subject, defines leadership as the control and integration of three elements – the task, the team and the individuals on the team. The role of the leader is therefore to motivate the individuals to come together as a team to complete the task in hand.

Discussion points

1 What are some of the characteristics of a good leader?

2 Can you think of any examples of strong, 'natural' leaders?

3 Do you agree with the old saying that 'leaders are born, not made'?

Leaders or managers?

Leadership and management are very different roles and require very different people, according to Professional Abraham Zaleznik of Harvard Business School. Managers are essentially *administrators*, he believes, who motivate people to meet the company's objectives. Leaders, on the other hand, are *visionaries*, challenging existing practices and capable of motivating people to create and follow *new* objectives.

This does not imply that one role is more valuable than the other. The chief executive at the top obviously needs to exhibit leadership in the sense of having a clear long-term vision of where the company is going, yet may not always be good at administration. Managers at the operating level, however, tend to be better at administration and managing resources.

In any case, managers today, whether they are **line managers**, responsible for the running of a particular department or section, or **staff managers**, responsible over all for an administrative function like personnel, need increasingly to demonstrate leadership in order to motivate their groups towards greater performance.

As John Adair points out in the *Director* interview, people's expectations are changing. 'People now look for a much higher level of leadership than before. They expect to be consulted; to be listened to; to be informed; to be kept in the picture; to be partners in the enterprise. Good leaders create that sense of being a team, of involvement and commitment.'

So how many of you could make good leaders? There's a lot talked today about charisma,' says John Adair, 'but the old definition of genius as 90 per cent perspiration and 10 per cent inspiration also holds true for leadership.' In other words, there is no substitute for hard work, energy and enthusiasm.

What does one of Britain's top chief executives look for in picking good people? Richard Giordano, non-executive chairman of The BOC Group, is quoted in *The New Elite* as stressing that 'You pick people by looking back at their records first of all . . . The second element I have learned the hard way. Make certain you pick people with a good set of personal qualities. I've had people who were probably intellectually below the salt. I've chosen employees who have been excessively defensive, bordering on dishonesty. They can't stand to see their mistakes in the light of day and have covered them up. I've had people who were just not articulate – brainy and all that, but hell on wheels to communicate with . . . Then there are some who just don't want to work!'

CASE STUDY

*Allied Lyons –
the mystery is
revealed*

For a company like Allied Lyons, with over 58,000 employees and 4,300 pubs in 1994 continuing success hinges directly on the standards of customer care set by the managers of those outlets. Maintaining or improving quality standards invariably involves a strong commitment to staff training, which in turn presumes that managers have some indication of where their strengths and weaknesses lie. The Mystery Customer Audit Scheme, devised by Allied's Retailing Sector as a means of measuring the standards achieved in their outlets, has proved an objective and extremely accurate method of assessment based on the all-important perspective of the customer. It is an approach that could have far-reaching implications for other firms operating at the sharp end of the service sector.

The impetus for the initiative derived from the need to ensure that the kind of hospitality and amenities being offered to customers were of a uniform standard throughout the company, and more importantly that they were of a comparable or better standard than those of rival breweries. Like all good ideas, the scheme is essentially very simple. All the pubs are visited periodically by the so-called 'Mystery Drinkers', who can be male or female, arrive alone or in groups and appear at any time during opening hours. Inspectors are drawn from an independent agency which ensures that they are impartial. The inspectors rate each outlet on the basis of a large number of objective factors covering interior and exterior cleanliness, together with the quality of welcome and service, range of amenities and condition of facilities.

All the factors which could conceivably affect why customers prefer one pub to another are covered with questions like, 'Was the internal decor well maintained?' 'Were you served within three minutes?' Were the drinks served at the right temperature?' 'Were the toilets clean?' Points are awarded for each answer from which an overall score is calculated. Two neighbouring pubs are also surveyed at the same time, which allows the pub to be judged against its major rivals. An incentive programme means that the managers of high-scoring pubs stand to win foreign holidays, country-house weekends and a host of other prizes.

In reality, of course, the scheme ultimately benefits all managers in that feedback from the assessment programme can be incorporated into a sharply focused training scheme. Armed with this information, managers can build on the strengths of their staff and address any areas of weakness that have been identified. In fact, subsequent analysis has shown that following each Mystery Customer Audit the average score for the company as a whole, relative to the competition, has increased significantly. In providing a revealing insight into standards as seen from the customer's point of view, the scheme has clearly enabled Allied's Retailing Sector to identify areas where competitive advantage may be gained.

What should management training include?

According to a report published in 1987, 'The Making of Managers', whose principal author was Professor Charles Handy, the extent of management training in the UK lags far behind that of its four main competitors.

The USA invests vast amounts in training. Japan has a compulsory system whereby managers have to go through a systematic process of self-education. In France, employers are required by law to spend a minimum annual sum on training for each employee. The Germans go through a long preparatory training and normally do not even start their managerial careers until they are at least 27 years old.

What should a good management training programme include? Sir Trevor Holdsworth, the former chairman of GKN, has reservations about some of the courses at management training centres being too academic. He is quoted in *The New Elite* as arguing (tongue in cheek!) that the best management training course would be one confined to three disciplines: chess, bridge and poker. 'Chess represents strategic thinking in a wider form, while bridge is working with a partner and poker is taking a calculated risk and having the nerve to see it through. All the elements of business management are captured in those three games.'

Apart from the courses run at business schools and management training centres, many UK companies do in fact offer their own training courses.

How do management styles vary?

The degree to which a manager gives responsibility for decision making can be ranked along a scale, as shown in the diagram on the next page.

At either end of the scale are the two styles of management – autocratic and democratic.

- **Autocratic** managers set objectives for the group, demonstrate their own authority, and expect orders to be obeyed blindly and without question. Communication is downward, so group members do not have the necessary information to make their own decisions. Such managers see workers as replaceable production units who can only be motivated by fear or by appeals to their self-interest in terms of money.
- **Democratic** managers, on the other hand, encourage group members to set their own objectives and delegate authority wherever possible, giving reasons for any orders or instructions they give out. Participation in decision making in encouraged and group members are given the necessary information to form these opinions, which the manager takes into account when making a final decision. This managerial style is based on workers being seen as human beings, who can be trusted to put their hearts into the task.

Research has shown that this last style results in the highest productivity, greatest feelings of involvement and job satisfaction and the best relations, though it does mean managers have to be good communicators and have to take time for the necessary consultation with workers.

However, a job-centred autocratic management style can also achieve high productivity, though groups managed like this tend to show dissatisfaction with their work and output is generally of lower quality. Such groups also experience greater conflict with management and suffer from a high turnover.

In any case, much research has also shown that managers do not adopt one style in all situations. The style adopted varies according to the manager's own personality, ability and experience and the personalities, skill and experience of the group members. The size of workforce, kind of job done and time available for completion are also influential. The nature of the organisation and the management style which have traditionally been used are important factors too.

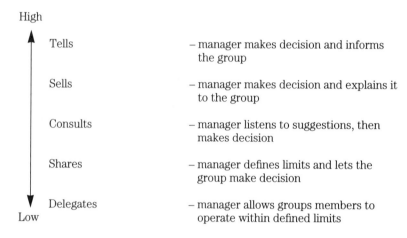

Scale of management styles

High

Tells — manager makes decision and informs the group

Sells — manager makes decision and explains it to the group

Consults — manager listens to suggestions, then makes decision

Shares — manager defines limits and lets the group make decision

Delegates — manager allows groups members to operate within defined limits

Low

Source: Tannebaum and Schmidt, *Harvard Business Review.*

ACTIVITY

Comparison of management styles

1 **1** Decide which type of management style would be most appropriate in the following situations:
   a) A group of unskilled workers engaged in completing a complex task.
   b) A group of inexperienced workers meeting a tight time deadline.
   c) A new manager appointed to run a division of a large firm, where consultative committees have traditionally existed.
   d) A group of skilled workers making high-quality products.
   e) A group of skilled employees in a small family firm.
   f) A large factory with hundreds of employees, when a fire breaks out.
   g) A new manager taking over an ailing company who needs to cut production costs, reduce staff and introduce financial controls.
   h) A group of inexperienced workers who believe management is paid to make decisions.
2 Why could you make a case for either style being appropriate in the situations in **g)** and **h)**?

Discussion points

1   Can one management style work best in most situations?

2   Which styles have been adopted by successful leaders that you can think of?

Management structures

Most companies have traditionally been organised on a **pyramid structure**, where employees at each level in the hierarchy are at a certain rank and have a particular role to fulfil in the organisation. In this kind of structure, there is a clearly defined **chain of command**. Orders tend to move downwards and the main flow of information is upwards.

At ICI a very steep pyramid existed, where it was calculated that there were as many as 16 layers of management between the shop floor and the chairman. As part of his recovery strategy for ICI, Sir John Harvey-Jones

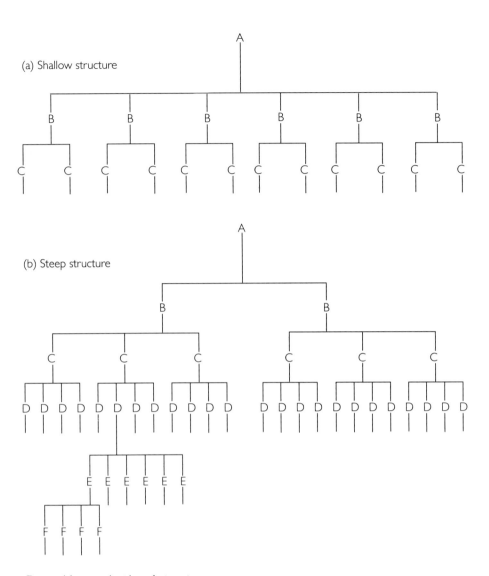

Pyramid organisational structure

pruned out many of these layers in order to revitalise the management structure.

Some companies are now organised instead on a **matrix structure**, where the authority for decision making is shifted down the organisation so that it lies with the heads of sections or of subsidiary companies, giving them more autonomy. Even a business organised on a traditional pyramid structure may use the matrix approach at times, when complex problems need to be solved quickly. For example, a team of people spanning different areas like production, personnel, finance and marketing, drawn from all levels in the organisation, may meet together to investigate a problem like poor quality control. A matrix structure such as this improves communication, speeds up decision making and encourages motivation through allowing employees greater opportunities for involvement and participation.

CASE STUDY

*Tetley Tea Bags –
winning round
the market*

Corporations such as Allied Lyons where the operational divisions or subsidiary companies are given a high degree of management autonomy invariably have an excellent record of product innovation. This is because managers at the operational level, being closer to the market, are in a better position to respond to consumer needs. The pace of change today is such that all firms need to introduce new products periodically in order to maintain their competitive edge. But for managers operating in the fast-moving consumer goods sector, the ability to read the market and introduce innovative products that successfully cater for new consumer needs has never been more important. In some cases, the results have been spectacular.

The introduction by Lyons Tetley, in 1989, of Tetley round tea bags provides a prime example. Compared to a figure of £64 million in 1989, by 1992, the brand was worth £111 million in the UK alone – representing an unprecedented increase for such a short space of time. The sales performance, which far exceeded the levels initially projected, prompted managers to expand round tea bags into overseas markets. In fact, the product has proved a winner in every country where it has been introduced. The commercial success mirrors that of the square tea bag, first introduced by Joseph Tetley back in 1953, which revolutionised the industry by enabling tea to compete with the convenience of instant coffee.

Management support for the Tetley brand, involving a five-year period of research and development costing £9 million, has clearly proved a worthwhile investment. Given the notoriously high failure rate of new products, with only 1 in 10 of those launched surviving their first three years in the marketplace, managers cannot take it for granted that they have a potential winner on their hands, despite the extensive market research that is done beforehand.

In the event, rapid consumer acceptance, backed by a massive advertising campaign featuring the popular 'Tetley Tea Folk' together with sales promotions such as a cash-back offer and the distribution of free samples, enabled Lyons Tetley to increase sales substantially and regain their market share (which had fallen from 23 per cent in 1980 to 15 per cent in 1988). Before long, Tetley round tea bags were vying with PG Tips for market leadership and today Tetley is the market leader. Underpinning this impressive performance are several factors – the product is innovative, clearly differentiated from competing products and has a strong brand identity. In the final analysis, however, the ability of managers to respond to changing consumer needs is undoubtedly the crucial factor determining success or failure.

Scene from a commercial for Tetley Tea Bags

Who makes decisions?

How is authority for decision making actually allocated in different organisations? In organisations with a **centralised management structure**, the majority of decisions are made by a few people. Those with a **decentralised management structure**, on the other hand, may give responsibility for decision making to senior managers in different divisions concerned with different product groups. Such a shifting or **delegation** of responsibility for decision making downwards through the organisation encourages greater motivation, because of the autonomy gained. This can be seen in the diagram showing Grand Metropolitan plc's organisation into divisions. With a turnover of almost 8.12 billion and in spite of employing over 87,163 people worldwide, Grand Metropolitan's headquarters employ less than 200 staff!

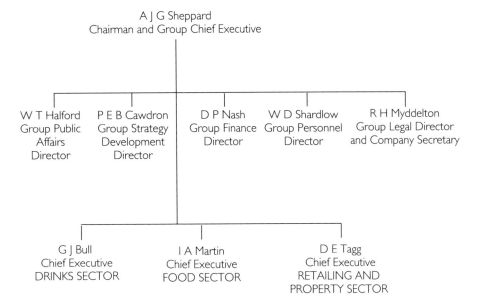

Grand Metropolitan Plc, organisation chart

A spectacular example of a company trying to shake itself free of head office bureaucracy occurred when Bob Horton, the former chairman of BP, was first appointed to that post. Within a week he announced that more than 1000 jobs would be cut from BP's massive headquarters in the City. With them went an elaborate hierarchical structure and about 70 committees, all supposedly needed to manage or coordinate the global business, but which were actually stifling initiative and action in the operating units.

Peters and Waterman highlighted the fact that the successful American companies they studied invariably split their operations into small, independent units. Each unit is allowed maximum freedom to operate except in certain key areas, which management feel are so important that they need centralised control over them.

In their description of 23 successful British companies which they identified as standing out from the corwd, Walter Goldsmith and David Clutterbuck, in their book *The Winning Streak*, found decentralised management structures were the norm. The only exceptions were the retailing chains and the Trust House Forte hotel chain, where a greater degree of central control is required to maintain uniform standards.

In describing the situation at Clarks, who operate in the shoe making industry, Goldsmith and Clutterbuck point out that 'The revelation came during World War Two, when the company had to give up its main factory for the production of torpedoes. The mass production halls were dispersed into numerous smaller buildings in the surrounding area. Productivity rose 250 per cent. Since then, Clarks has retained all its production in relatively small, semi-autonomous units.'

These authors also observe that the basic philospohy behind the success of the Racal Electronics Group is their policy of establishing small individual companies, with less than 500 employees, each responsible for the design, development and marketing of its own products. According to Sir Ernest Harrison, the former chairman of Racal Electronics, 'A small business has one product and a small team of people, who can be so intense in their interest that they get the best product and the best effort out of the people who work for them. . . . Everyone knows the costs, everyone knows the boss and everyone knows the customers.'

ACTIVITY

Decentralised management structure

Using the table below to help you, draw up a similar table listing the advantages and disadvantages of a decentralised management structure.

	Centralised management structure
Advantages	Senior management provided with information from all parts of the organisation, so are in a good position to make decisions.
	Senior management can be expected to make better decisions than more junior staff with less experience.
	Less time spent in coordinating activities of different divisions or departments.
	Managers can ensure uniform standards are met.
	Succeeds well in an organisation with an autocratic management structure.
Disadvantages	Senior management may be inundated with more information than they can absorb or have the time deal with.
	Junior and middle managers have fewer opportunities to gain experience, as decision making is restricted to senior management.
	Decisions may take longer to make as information is relayed to managers through people at different levels in the organisation.
	More expensive because of the administrative systems which need to be set up when the organisation is controlled from the centre.
	Senior management may lose touch with operating conditions through being several layers of management removed from 'grass roots'.

CASE STUDY

Virgin – effective management in action

Pick up any newspaper or magazine and there's a good chance you'll come across a picture of Richard Branson sporting his irrepressible toothy grin and trademark woolly jumper. Airline owner, daredevil stunt man and entrepreneur extraordinaire, few businessmen have captured the public imagination as completely as the larger-than-life chairman of Virgin. The press have elevated him to the status of folk hero, reporting his hot-air balloon and speedboat exploits with relish and devoting endless column inches to each new business venture.

Branson's earliest business venture was in fact as the publisher of a student magazine when he was still a 16-year-old schoolboy. However, the real break came when, in a bid to raise cash for the financially-strapped magazine, he hit on the idea of selling discounted records by mail order. The initial advertisement produced a flood of responses and he was soon able to open his first Oxford Street record shop in 1971. The purchase of a recording studio in 1972 proved a huge success when the first album released – Tubular Bells by Mike Oldfield – went on to sell five million copies. At the age of 23, Branson had made his first million. In the years since, artists like Janet Jackson, Culture Club, Human League, Phil Collins and Paula Abdul helped to turn the music division into one of the most successful record labels in the world. Branson later pulled off the deal of a lifetime when the sale of Virgin Music to Thorn EMI in 1992 netted the company a cool £560 million.

In the space of 25 years Branson has built a major entertainment empire with a turnover of £1.4 billion and 7,500 employees in 150 operating companies. Virgin interests around the world, as they are now, consist of five holding companies: Travel, Retail, Communications, Hotels and Investments. The two major divisions are Virgin Travel, which is dominated by the airline, and Virgin Retail which operates music and entertainment stores, including the Megastores chain. So what are the management principles governing the company whose growth has been almost entirely self-generated, with only a handful of acquisitions and partnership deals?

Branson's management philosophy rests squarely on the 'small is beautiful' principle put forward by the economist EF Schumacher. According to Schumacher, it is only when a large organisation is broken down into many small autonomous units, that the proper balance between freedom, which promotes creativity, and order, which gets things done, can be maintained. As Branson says, 'Once people stop knowing the other people in the building, it's time to break up a company into smaller units. The ideal size is around 50 to 60 people. By keeping a company small, you give more people a chance.'

Richard Branson

In line with this philosophy, the highly decentralised management structure that has evolved at Virgin is a classic example of 'empowerment', with managers being given the freedom to organise the day-to-day running of their companies as they see fit. As one manager points out, 'He'll sometimes disagree with you but then says, "Go ahead, you're the boss" '. The fact that many of the top executives have been with the company since it started is perhaps the best proof that managers appreciate being given the room to follow their own judgement.

Staff turnover is also low. So what factors explain this loyalty? 'We're an entertainment company so things are done slightly differently to other companies', admits Branson. 'We don't have a clock in, clock out mentality. Because of this climate, people are quite willing to work long hours.' Based on the principle that people feel more motivated when they have a stake in the company's future, 85 per cent of promotions are internal appointments. Other key factors include the use of incentive payment schemes and the fact that employees have the option of buying shares in the company. In fact, well over a dozen of the top managers at Virgin are now millionaires in their own right.

Branson has clearly fostered a winning management style at Virgin, delegating authority to his managers whilst leaving himself free to do what he does best – coming up with ideas for new ventures and getting them off the ground.

FINAL ACTIVITY

Jinx Games Ltd: 'all in a day's work!'

DALEFORD FOOTBALL CLUB

127 The Links
DALEFORD
OF7 2AL

Mrs Helen Robinson   September 9th
Jinx Games Ltd.
DALEFORD
DF3 4BH

Dear Mrs Robinson,
    We will be holding our annual disco at the end of next month at 8.30 p.m. on October 28th.
    As you have very kindly sponsored us this year, we wondered if you would come along and present the cups to the winning players? I look forward to hearing from you.

Yours sincerely,

Kenneth Jameson

Kenneth Jameson
(Club Secretary)

☎
PHONE MESSAGES
1. Factory foreman rang. Would like to discuss his prospects in the company. Has had another job offer and needs to give them an answer by next weekend.
2. Finance controller rang. Customer owing £20,000 gone into receivership. He thinks another consignment of goods is to be dispatched to them today.
3. Reporter from 'Derbyshire Business Review' rang. Would like an interview for an article in next week's issue.
4. Buyer from Jarrods department store rang. Goods due to be delivered a week ago not arrived yet.

BACKGROUND TO THE COMPANY

Jinx Games Ltd is a manufacturer of board games, located in the small town of Daleford in the Pennines. The company employs 40 people, has a turnover of £1.8 million and is regarded locally as a reputable and well-run firm. Sales are seasonal and the firm gets especially busy in the run-up to Christmas. The company gets orders steadily from small toy shops round the country, but their biggest orders tend to be from the major department stores in the cities.

The firm was started eight years ago by Helen Robinson, who is the managing director. On this particular Friday in September, Helen arrives in the office at 10.30 a.m., after a meeting with one of the suppliers, to find on her desk a list of phone messages from her secretary together with a letter which arrived this morning. She also has a list of things written down in her diary to deal with today.

DECIDING PRIORITIES

Put yourself in the position of Helen Robinson. Having read the phone messages, letter and diary entries, decide how **urgent** and how **important** each situation is.

1. Make a list of the order in which you have to deal with each situation. (Plan the possible combinations in rough first.)
2. By the side of each item on your list, state which managerial role you are carrying out in dealing with each situation. (Refer back to the diagram of roles identified by Mintzberg on p.95.)

ACTION REQUIRED   Friday September 13th

1. Write memo informing everyone the company Christmas 'do' will this year be held at 'Marco and Luigi's' on December 15th.
2. Arrange to see 'Platt and Margate' insurance brokers to update insurance policies which will run out at the end of the month.
3. Look at budget figures to decide where the money for advertising the new game to be launched in two months' time is to be drawn from.
4. Ring 'Apollo Computers' to arrange for a representative to visit and discuss the computerisation of the company accounts system.
5. Arrange meeting with Sales Manager to review last month's sales figures.

Jinx Games Ltd: Helen Robinson's desk

Small Business

Introduction: the small firms revival

How small is small? Definitions vary, from the 'under 24 employees' stated by the Small Business Research Trust, to the measure adopted by the Department of Employment, which classifies small firms in manufacturing as being those with fewer than 200 employees. However, an accepted formula seems to be that described in the 1981 Companies Act. This defines a small firm as being one which during any accounting year does not exceed *two* of the following criteria: turnover of £1.4 million, total assets of £0.7 million, workforce of 50 employees.

The 1993 *Size Analysis of UK Businesses* showed that 89 per cent of all manufacturing firms are small firms of under 50 employees, accounting for 24 per cent of manufacturing employment. In fact, 66 per cent of all manufacturing firms were very small firms of under nine employees. Only 3 per cent of manufacturing firms have more than 200 employees!

In the post-war period of economic growth, small businesses were widely regarded as being inefficient. Only large firms could afford to adopt all the latest technological developments and improve their productivity by making huge economies of scale. The impact of such attitudes was confirmed by the government-commissioned Bolton Report, published in 1971, which concluded that, 'The small firms sector is in a state of long-term decline.' However, the Report argued that small firms (which they defined as having fewer than 200 employees) fulfilled an important role in the economy, by creating jobs and stimulating competition and innovation. Some of the measures recommended by the Report, such as the setting up of a Small Firms Service, were later adopted.

Since 1971, there has been a dramatic increase in the numbers of small firms. Why is this so? What advantages do small firms offer over larger firms? The UK's SMEs (small and medium enterprises) are estimated to have accounted for two-thirds of private sector employment and 75–100 per cent of net job creation in recent times, whereas during the 1980s the larges companies reduced their collective workforce by over 1.3 million. Unlike large firms, which are tending to shed jobs, small firms are creating jobs and thus stimulating economic growth.

In addition, their small scale of operations means that they do not face the same problems as larger firms, many of which are associated with production-line work. Due to their closeness to the market, they also tend to be more in touch with market trends. They can be more flexible in responding to changing market demands, because they are owner managed and so decisions can be taken quickly. They generally tend to be more innovative and, because they often provide highly specialised products and services, are seen as being important in providing consumers with a greater choice.

Apart from the advantages inherent in their small size, there are various economic, social and political factors which have encouraged the small firms revival.

Table 8.1 *Why are there more small firms today?*

Service industries	As the service sector of the economy has increased dramatically in recent years, more opportunities have been created for small firms. Service firms, being labour intensive, can be started with very little capital outlay, unlike manufacturing firms which need heavy initial outlays on plant and equipment.
Standards of living	More small firms are starting up as general standards of living have risen. These have exploited new markets catering for the specialised products and services demanded by consumers with higher disposable incomes.
Redundancies and unemployment	Many of the workers made redundant as a result of their firms closing down or cutting back have decided to start up small firms, especially if they live in areas where their chances of finding another job are slim. Similarly, many unemployed people have decided to set up their own business, as an alternative to the dole queues.
Opportunities for subcontracting	Large firms prefer to subcontract out limited production runs or specialised services where the work is not profitable for their scale of operations. This creates opportunities for small firms to survive in the **sheltered market** created. Opportunities increase in times of fierce competition, which causes large firms to concentrate even more on their core or principal activities.
Government encouragement	Small firms are widely recognised as creating jobs, stimulating economic growth and avoiding many of the labour problems larger firms face. As a result, most governments have actively encouraged the formation of small firms in recent decades.

Why do some industries have many small firms?

Richard Scase and Robert Goffee, in their book *The Real World of the Small Business Owner*, describe four conditions which encourage small manufacturing firms to grow up. These include:

- **Labour intensiveness**. The textile, footwear and printing and publishing industries provide many opportunities for small firms. They are all traditional industries that depend on most work being done by hand rather than by machine.
- **Subcontracting**. The engineering industry sustains large numbers of small firms, who survive by supplying the specialised goods and services which large firms subcontract out.
- **Technological innovation**. The plastics, instrument engineering and electronic engineering industries are all areas where small firms have grown up making the innovative products which have been developed.
- **Market variability**. The furniture and clothing industries and the manufacture of various domestic items are all consumer goods industries which offer **market niches** for new businesses, catering for particular fashions or specialised items.

Of these factors, Scase and Goffee conclude that 'labour intensiveness is perhaps the most important since the initial capital requirements for start up purposes tend to be low'.

ACTIVITY

Percentage of employees in small firms found in each manufacturing industry

On your copy of the table below, write down the percentage of small firms in each manufacturing industry. Which industries have the highest concentration of small firms?

Manufacturing industries (standard industrial classification)	Total number of employees in small firms (under 50 employees)	Total number of employees in each industrial sector	Percentage of employees in small firms within each industrial sector
Chemical industry and production of synthetic fibres	28,967	258,582	
Manufacture of metal goods	112,109	288,845	
Mechanical engineering	180,627	524,627	
Manufacture of office machinery and data processing equipment	9,401	53,990	
Electrical and electronic engineering	70,991	450,029	
Manufacture of motor vehicles and parts	19,312	223,749	
Manufacture of other transport equipment	15,091	240,475	
Instrument engineering	20,848	77,919	
Food, drink & tobacco manufacturing industries	75,350	520,297	
Textile industry	32,651	169,985	
Manufacture of leather and leather goods	6,902	15,034	
Footwear and clothing	66,683	228,878	
Timber and wooden furniture industries	83,790	179,111	
Manufacture of paper and paper products, printing and publishing	151,967	432,945	
Processing of rubber and plastics	56,330	222,495	

Source: Central Statistical Office, *Size Analysis of UK Businesses* 1993, Table 7a.

Why do people set up in business?

Becoming an **entrepreneur** involves undertaking a risk in a commercial venture. What factors motivate the ever increasing flood of people to risk going it alone? The 'Enterprise in Britain' study of almost 6,000 small business owners and self-employed people showed that the age at which most people start up is between 30 and 40, when they have the work experience, access to capital (with mortgages easier and children growing up) and necessary motivation (if promotion does not materialise).

Dissatisfaction with being an employee is undoubtedly the trigger for many, especially if there is no challenge or job satisfaction left in their present jobs and prospects of promotion are limited. Running a business can provide an attractive alternative to being stuck on the company ladder, with the opportunity to make decisions, take on responsibility and enjoy what is for many entrepreneurs the main benefit – the ability to control their own destiny. Some employees may decide in time to put their skills and abilities to use making profits for themselves, rather than for the organisation they have been with. Those who are at a disadvantage in the labour market because of discrimination, such as ethnic minority groups, also find business start-ups attractive.

Similarly, according to Robert Goffee and Richard Scase in their book *Women in Charge*, a growing number of women are starting their own businesses to avoid the frustration of limited career prospects. 'To a large extent this is because senior male managers continue to query their ability to occupy top corporate positions. Some are concerned about the supposed psychological and emotional qualities of women, others are anxious about their organisational "commitment". As a result, there may be a reluctance to train or promote women. By starting their own business women can achieve the material success and personal ambitions denied them in large organisations.'

People may also be tempted to become entrepreneurs through deciding to develop an innovative idea for a product or service that they have come up with, but which their present company does not regard as commercially viable. David Oates, in his book *The Complete Entrepreneur*, quotes the case of Robert Mann, who stumbled on an idea for a fire protection product he was sure would sell well. The product was based on a material which is inset as a thin strip in vulnerable areas such as door frames. If a fire occurs the material expands under the heat, sealing off the gap in the frames and preventing the fire spreading. The chemical group he was working for at the time thought the product was too specialised and was unlikely to generate a big enough sales volume to justify the necessary investment. However, the firm agreed to support him by supplying him with the raw material at a good price and also helped him with credit. Within just five years, Mann's company was exporting worldwide and had a turnover of £400,000.

In some cases, people have become entrepreneurs because they have discovered a gap or niche in a particular market through wanting to use a product or service, finding it does not exist and then deciding to manufacture or supply it themselves. Others seek to provide an existing product or service for a gap which they have identified in a local or regional market. Less often than is commonly thought, small businesses are founded by those who manage to invent a completely new product or service, thus stimulating a new demand. Sometimes entrepreneurs can discover a useful product which is not widely available and set up a company themselves to market it more extensively.

Changing personal circumstances, such as being made redundant, can often be a powerful spur, with the redundancy lump sum providing some of the finance needed. However, evidence suggests that businesses started by individuals who have been pushed into start-ups by negative reasons have a lower growth rate than businesses started by those who have become entrepreneurs for positive reasons, such as identifying a gap in the market or coming up with an idea for a new product.

The trend towards increasing numbers of **management buy-outs** in recent years shows no sign of slowing down. This is where the managers buy out the company they are working for, or a division of it, and then run it as an independent concern. The impetus for taking this step is often the threat of closure. Buy-outs have tended to be very successful, on the whole, largely because the management team who already have experience of running the company stays in place. Finance is easier to obtain for such ventures because they are already a going concern, so constitute less risk for investors than completely new start-ups.

Whatever the motivating factors, with the 'enterprise culture' that exists in Britain today and the degree of help and advice available, conditions for starting up a small business have never been more favourable. The first step for any new entrepreneur is to prepare a detailed business plan on all aspects of the proposed venture, in order to assess whether the idea is commercially viable.

ACTIVITY

The lending quiz

How would a bank rate your business plan?

On your copy of the questions below, tick the answer which you think is most appropriate for each question. When you have finished, add up the scores for each answer, given on your teacher's scoring sheet, to determine **your** credit rating.

1   You are writing your own business plan to apply for a bank loan to start up a small business. Do you:
   a) include a short paragraph outlining your background and career so far?
   b) include a detailed profile of yourself giving full details of your previous relevant experience, work achievements, training and education?
   c) leave out any details about yourself as this is less relevant than the sales projections and cash-flow forecasts you have included?

2   You are able to raise as personal finance, through a variety of sources, a percentage of the start-up finance required. Do you contribute:
   a) 10 per cent?
   b) 20 per cent?
   c) 40 per cent?

3   You are assessing the likely size and nature of potential demand for your products. Do you:
   a) carry out an informal survey amongst friends and family?
   b) commission a well-known, reputable market research agency to carry out a detailed survey?
   c) obtain any previously published survey results for similar products and carry out some field research for a small sample?

4   You are deciding how to plan the marketing most efficiently. Do you:
   a) carry out test marketing in order to decide how to use adverts, leaflets etc. in a logical sequence?
   b) commission a well-known and reputable advertising agency to test-market your products?
   c) avoid wasting scarce start-up resources on test marketing, as you already know what products you want to sell and how you need to market them?

5   You are deciding which bank to approach for start-up finance. Do you:
   a) approach a new bank as you think it is going to be more receptive than your own, giving them a complete set of bank statements for the last three years, showing satisfactory account behaviour?
   b) approach your own bank with which you have banked satisfactorily for five years?

CREDIT RATING

Final score

30 or   Your loan application is certain to be approved as it is well
more   prepared and thorough.

24–29   Your loan application is likely to be approved though some
         areas will need a bit more attention to detail.

18–23   You need to go away and prepare a more carefully thought-
         out business plan, if you wish the application to go through.

Under   You need to think again about whether there is any point in
18   your going into business on your own.

ACTIVITY

Factors considered by a bank manager when assessing a business plan

The questions that follow are adapted from Barclays Small Business pack for small firms.
Which of the factors do you think a bank manager would assess most carefully in each of the following key areas of a business plan?

*   Background of entrepreneur
*   Background of business
*   Products or services
*   Markets and sales
*   Financial considerations
*   When will break-even point be reached?
*   Has the entrepreneur any relevant experience in this field?
*   Have the strengths which make the business competitive in the market been identified?
*   Can the repayments be met on the amount borrowed?
*   What will happen if the key personnel are unable to work?
*   Has a target market been identified?
*   Are premises adequate for future needs?
*   How much of his/her own capital is the entrepreneur prepared to put in?
*   What are the entrepreneur's business objectives, and how practical are they?
*   Have the core or principal products or services been identified?
*   Is the level of projected sales realistic?
*   Who are the key suppliers and how much trade credit will they allow?
*   Is the choice of premises suitable, in terms of size, location and cost, for the type of business?
*   What percentage does each product or service contribute to turnover?
*   How will prices be calculated?
*   Does the cash flow forecast include a reasonable margin of error?
*   Is the market declining, static or increasing, and why?
*   How detailed is the breakdown of expenditure?
*   Who are the major competitors?
*   Is the cash flow forecast realistic and detailed enough?
*   Has the entrepreneur any recognised business training?
*   Has any market research been carried out?
*   Has the entrepreneur already got any firm orders?
*   What methods of marketing will be used?
*   What insurance cover will be taken out?
*   Does the planned expenditure take into account future growth?
*   Is the general character of the entrepreneur suitable for running a business?
*   Can the business obtain any grants?

Phil's business plan

'Phil Davies, isn't it? Good to see you. I'm John Woodford, the manager of this branch. Do take a seat. I understand from the business plan which you sent me that you would like a Barclays Business Starter loan of £10,000, to set up a small business.'

'Yes, that's right. I want to set up a business making a range of small leather gifts. You see, I've had a lot of experience in the leather trade and I'm sure I can make a go of it if I work hard enough.'

'Fine. But I think it would perhaps be helpful if we could go through the plan now, as there are some areas which you might want to consider in more detail, before the loan application is assessed by the bank. I see that you've been with Classic Leather Goods for the last 12 years, as assistant production manager. Are you still with them?'

'No, actually I leave at the end of this month. I decided it was time I went, having just been passed over for promotion for the second time. I was ready for a change anyway. Who needs all that aggravation? I just want to be my own boss from now on, with no one telling me how I should do my job or breathing down my neck all the time.'

'I see, but do you have any capital to invest in the business?'

'Well, there's quite a lot, almost a thousand I think, in my savings account, though I want to use that to tide me over the first few months. Anyway, the profits will be rolling in soon from all the different products I plan to make, so after a year or so I'll be fine.'

'You mentioned making a lot of different products. Are there any products you would concentrate on making, which would form the core of your business?'

'Not really. I thought originally I would just make wallets, purses and credit-card holders, but then I decided to make a complete range of gifts – everything from leather photograph frames to desk sets. After all, people always want something a bit out of the ordinary, don't they?'

'Oh, have you done some market research, then?'

'There wasn't much point really. Classic Leather always seemed to make good profits, and anyway people always need to buy presents, especially around Christmas time.'

'That's certainly true. But even if the overall size of market demand is good, why should consumers choose your products rather than anyone else's? Do your products have any strengths or special features which will make them stand out from the crowd?'

'Well, I thought that as a small business I could afford to charge lower prices, because my expenses and running costs are lower, so that way I can undercut the competition because my products will be cheaper.'

'The trouble is, you can come unstuck trying to compete solely on the basis of price with firms who produce in volume, because they can cut their costs right down by making economies of scale. It would be far better if you could compete with the big firms by offering better quality products, or specialise by making something they don't. During your time at Classic Leather, perhaps you noticed a gap in the market which is not being catered for as yet?'

'No, I can't say I have. I thought I would stick to making the same sort of gifts, just sell them more cheaply. I can get the materials I need quite a bit cheaper if I pay cash in advance. I haven't actually got any firm orders yet, but once I get going, I won't have any trouble meeting those sales projections figures. After all, good products sell themselves, don't they? I'm certainly not going to waste any money on marketing to begin with. The main thing is for me to spend time going round all the stores and gift shops with my samples. Later on, I might get a few leaflets printed up or put some ads in a trade magazine.'

'Though of course your cash flow forecasts do depend on meeting the level of sales you predict. Does your planned expenditure include a margin of safety, in case you don't manage to sell as much as you hoped?'

'Oh, I'm sure there'll be absolutely no problem in selling the amounts I quoted. Anyway, so long as the business ticks over, I'll be quite happy – I'm not bothered about making millions!'

'Well, you will certainly need to look carefully at whether the business will generate enough profit to cover your own salary, which has to meet your mortgage and other commitments, before you decide whether or not to proceed with this venture.'

'I see. But surely if you're prepared to work hard and your products are much cheaper than everyone else's, you can't go wrong, can you?'

ACTIVITY

Assessing Phil's business plan

1 Using the list in the previous activity as a guide, state all the ways in which you would consider Phil's approach and business plan inadequate, if you were the bank manager.

2 Are there any areas in which you would rate Phil well?

3 In pairs, role play how 'you' think the conversation should have gone.

Raising the finance to start up

Most entrepreneurs struggle hard to raise the start-up capital needed for all the one-off purchases like machinery or premises, together with the working capital needed to pay for everyday running costs such as a stock of materials, wages, overheads and so on. Though preoccupied with survival and trying to keep their heads above water, their thoughts might occasionally stray to the day when their business takes off to the point where it starts to make millions and becomes a major household name. Just a pipe dream? Perhaps, yet the dream does become a reality for some.

The founding of Apple, the US-based computer firm, illustrates the kind of rags-to-riches success story which inspires many hard-pressed entrepreneurs to keep going when they might otherwise be tempted to give up. In common with the majority of small business start-ups, Apple began life on a shoestring budget.

The company was founded in 1977 by Steve Jobs and his partner Steve Wozniak. They began working from a garage, having sold some of their belongings to raise their start-up capital of $1,300. A shop owner liked their design drawings for the second version of their computer so much that he placed an order for 50 computers straight away. But this large order created problems because it meant they could not afford to buy the electronic parts they needed. In fact, they eventually obtained the $20,000's worth of parts needed from a supplier on a 30-day-trade credit basis – and managed to pay it all back in 29 days with the cash they got from the sale of the 50 computers.

However, things might well have gone wrong. If they had not been able to manufacture and deliver the computers within 30 days, or if the customer had been late paying them, the story might have been very different. In the event, the company went from strength to strength. Within the next four years, sales multiplied 430 times, according to one estimate.

Entrepreneurs generally have some of their own capital to invest, from savings, for instance, or a second mortgage on their home. Just how easy is it for small businesses to borrow money today? The high street clearing banks are by far the most important source of initial finance. They tend to have a reputation for being conservative, preferring safe rather than **speculative investments** – mainly because they are, after all, responsible to their own depositors, whose savings they are investing.

Most advances are based on the concept of **shared risk**, where only about 50 or 60 per cent of the capital required is lent. Investors want to see the entrepreneur put in the rest, partly as a gesture of good faith (if you are unwilling to risk your own money, why should they?), and partly because they would expect even greater effort and commitment if some of the entrepreneur's own capital is at stake. This principle is also adopted in the government's **Enterprise Allowance Scheme**, where people who have been unemployed are given £40 a week for a year when they start up a business, conditional on them already having or being able to borrow £1,000 themselves.

Lenders also require **security** to recover their loan should the business fail, the **collateral** often being provided in the form of the entrepreneur's own home. The government's **Loan Guarantee Scheme** is useful because it enables a loan to be granted in situations where it might otherwise not be; for instance, where inadequate security or the lack of an established track record makes the proposition unattractive to lenders. The government guarantees 70 per cent (85 per cent in some inner city areas) of a loan made by banks or financial institutions, up to a maximum of £100,000, thus enabling small businesses to provide the security lenders require. The small firm pays a 2.5 per cent premium to the government for the guarantee, which adds to the cost of borrowing. The scheme is now administered by the Training and Enterprise Councils (TECs).

In addition, small businesses can obtain finance through schemes such as **LINC**. Run by 14 Enterprise Agencies, this is a nationwide business introduction service which functions essentially as a 'marriage service'. Details of the small firms seeking capital are published in a monthly bulletin and investors can contact the firms which interest them via the box numbers given. Small firms can also raise finance through the European Investment Bank (EIB), which advances funds to banks and financial institutions which then lend on to small businesses. In the UK, this loan arrangement is carried out by Barclays Bank and 3i.

CASE STUDY

Richer pickings – a sound success

Who is the busiest retailer in Britain? Marks & Spencers? Sainsbury perhaps, or Tesco? Wrong on all three counts. The answer is Richer Sounds, a little known, privately owned, cut price retailer of hi-fi equipment with 13 shops in the UK. In this year's *Guinness Book of Records*, Richer Sounds warrants an entry for the highest sales per square foot of any retailer in the UK – £17,553 – for its store on London Bridge Walk in the City.

It is profitable too. Last year Richer Sounds made profits of more than £1.8 million on sales of £20 million. By contrast, Dixons made virtually nothing on retail sales. The man behind the company's success is founder, chairman and 100 per cent shareholder Julian Richer, a 35-year-old Londoner. In simple terms, the company sells discounted hi-fi from tiny basic shops with low overheads. Stock turnover is rapid and the company's small size gives it flexibility to take advantage of deals offered by manufacturers on end-of-line or surplus equipment. The technique has enabled Richer Sounds to secure itself a lucrative niche in a £4 billion audio visual market dominated by independents.

Suppliers are keen to do business with this quirky retailing operation. 'People like Dixons and Comet have so many stores (900 and 300 respectively) that unless you've got 5,000 of a model it's not worth their while putting it into their distribution system', says Clyde Roberts, sales and marketing director of Akai. 'With Richer, you can do a deal on 30.'

Kevin Harrington, regional sales manager with Sony, agrees. 'With a small management team they can make decisions quickly.' Marketing is a key weapon. Richer Sounds advertises regularly in national newspapers ('We buy late space at a discount,' Richer says) and in alternative magazines such as *Private Eye* and *Viz*.

The shops are like walk-in warehouses. And prices are cheap. Low prices are possible because fixed costs (rents and rates) are kept to a minimum – 2 per cent of turnover. The shops are tiny and in secondary locations, so that rents are low. Shop fittings are basic – no carpets and no fancy lighting.

Good service is another priority. At Richer Sounds staff are trained not to be pushy. First time hi-fi buyers get a call to check that they are happy with the equipment. Customer receipts include a freephone number they can dial if they have a problem. Richer's own name and office number are supplied too.

The emphasis is on fun. If it is raining, customers are given a free umbrella. In summer they get an ice lolly. Other seasonal gifts include mince pies at Christmas and hot cross buns at Easter. 'We have a laugh,' Richer says. 'We don't take ourselves seriously, but we do take our customers seriously.'

Richer's treatment of his staff – or 'colleagues' as he calls them – is reminiscent of Marks & Spencer (where his parents met as young employees). Fifteen per cent of profits are distributed to staff in a profit-share scheme. A further 1 per cent goes to a staff hardship fund for use in case of crisis, and 4 per cent goes to charity. Harley Street advice is available free of charge. Incentives are unusual. In addition to the standard carrot of company cars – the best 2 performing branches each month get free use of a Bentley for four weeks. 'I think it's great, but my insurance broker is not so sure', Richer jokes.

With 19 shops, good profits and a burgeoning reputation, Richer seems well placed to expand his niche. But, aware that this year's fastest growers are often next year's receiverships, he says he is not going to open shops on every high street. 'I'd like to cover every major conurbation and that would mean about 25 or 30 shops,' he says. 'But I'm not in a hurry. Things that are built slowly last longer.'

The Bentley Brooklands, one of the perks for the best-performing branches of Richer Sounds (Photograph reproduced by kind permission of Rolls Royce Motor Cars Limited)

Surviving in the market place

No matter how innovative the product or service offered by a small business, it will not become a commercially viable proposition unless it is marketable. The marketing methods which are used will be ineffective unless a gap in the market is exploited or a new demand is created by the product or service. Small firms are at an advantage in being more aware of changing trends, which they can respond to more easily than larger firms because of being flexible. It is usually far better for a small business to cater for specialised segments of the market, rather than to try to compete with large companies for the majority market.

Many new ventures are started by entrepreneurs who have been working in a particular industry and have spotted a need which is not being catered for. Airdata Ltd was founded in 1986 by two former Dan Air Pilots. They devised a sophisticated flight-planning program which is aimed at smaller airlines and can be run on microcomputers, unlike the alternative systems which need an expensive mainframe computer. Their system can plan routes, calculate fuel requirements, compare the cost of fuel in different countries to decide where refuelling should take place and automatically file flight plans with air traffic control.

Charles Steel of Airdata

The software is far more sophisticated than previous microcomputer systems, as it uses the Meteorological Office's grid for wind speed and strength. Airlines have such confidence in the accuracy of the system, which won a Design Council Award in 1988, that they have been able to use the program to reduce the amount of fuel carried on certain flights, resulting in dramatic cost savings. The Derbyshire-based firm has also won a SMART award (Small firms Merit Award for Research and Technology) from the Department of Trade and Industry. The firm has clearly exploited successfully a requirement which was not being filled.

CASE STUDY

Derwent Valley –
ingredients in
success

The name came up at about 10 o'clock one night in a pub in downtown Newcastle after we'd rejected 120 to 130 during that day – Phileas Fogg and his Fine Foods from Around the World', says Roger McKechnie, chairman of Derwent Valley Food Group. Phileas Fogg snacks have become widely established since Roger and three other directors founded the company in 1982. The initital target projection in their start-up business plan was to reach a turnover of £1 million in three years. Instead they achieved £5.5 million. Growth since then has been equally impressive.

The creation of 260 jobs at their factory in Consett, County Durham, has been especially worthwhile, as it has taken place in an area depressed by the closure of the local steelworks and the steady decline of traditional manufacturing industries, and with unemployment levels running as high as 28 per cent. Derwent Valley's growth provides an inspiration for other would-be entrepreneurs thinking of setting up a business away from the South East. Success has also won them numerous awards, including the prestigious CBI Company of the Year award in 1986.

Three of the four founder directors had all worked in the snacks industry. There they had noticed that, though children were catered for by concept-related snacks such as Monster Munch, there was a gap in the market for sophisticated snacks aimed at adults who, when entertaining at home, wanted something more exciting than the standard crisps or peanuts. To find new products, the four travelled the world, bringing back suitcases laden with snacks from which they narrowed the choice down to four: Mexican Tortilla Chips, Californian Corn Chips, Mignons Morceaux Croutons from France and Shanghai Nuts from China. New products have since been added to the range such as Bagel Chips, Pakoras and Punjab Puris.

Scene from an advertising campaign for Phileas Fogg Extra Hot Tortilla Chips

The company was initially based in a workshop leased from the British Steel Corporation. Says McKechnie, 'We were given a hut surrounded by barbed wire at the back of the old steel works at Consett. We called it Stalag 17! So there we were, having sold the idea, with no product and no machinery. And within six months we had to find the money.' In the event, a financial start-up package was arranged, with the help of the local Development Agency. Half the start-up capital – half a million pounds – was provided by 3i plc (Investors in Industry), along with a leasing arrangement for the plant and machinery. According to McKechnie, '3i claim they invest in people and they checked us out very hard. They put each of us, individually and together, through an interview the like of which I had never had in my life. But actually they then put in complimentary reports about us. Once a degree of confidence had developed between us, they were very supportive.'

Having got off the ground and started production, the next stage was to target the marketing effort at the unexploited niche which had been identified, namely adults who entertained at home and had sophisticated tastes. No attempt was made to cater for the majority market, which would have meant competing with larger companies for volume sales.

In line with the upmarket positioning of the Phileas Fogg range, which retails at double the price of other snacks, standards of quality are high. Natural flavours are used, even though these are much more expensive than the price of artificial flavours, and the packaging incorporates expensive metallised laminate, which extends the shelf-life of the products.

The design element of the packet itself was critical. It had to act as advertising and look appealing on the shelf because the new company could not afford the expense of advertising in the early days. Overheads were also kept low by using the services of a network of distributors in the early stages, to avoid the cost of maintaining a nationwide sales force.

The company has now diversified into other product ranges including the Tapas range of chip and dip snacks. It also supplies own-label snacks to such leading names as Marks & Spencer and Sainsbury's. Its products are exported widely and its turnover is currently at more than £24 million. 'In February 1993 the company was bought by United Biscuits, Britain's largest manufacturer of biscuits and snacks, for an estimated £24 million.'

ACTIVITY

Ranking of ingredients of success in new ventures

On your individual copy of the table below, rank each ingredient of success in new ventures in order of importance from 1 to 10, and write the ranking in your column. Rank the ingredient you rate as being most important as 1, through to the least important as 10. Collect the rankings of other members in your group onto your table. Add the figures across and fill in the column for the group's total ranking. The **lowest** total (nearest to 5) is the most important ingredient, the next lowest the second most important, and so on. What do your results reveal?

Ingredients of success in new ventures	Group member 1	Group member 2	Group member 3	Group member 4	Total ranking for group	Final order of importance
Having relevant experience of the industry.						
Identifying an unexploited gap in the market.						
Creating a new need by offering an innovative product or service.						
Catering for a specialised part of the market, rather than for the majority market.						
Directing marketing at the target market.						
Keeping overheads low in the early stages.						
Having enough cash to meet requirements for working capital.						
Ensuring interest charges and loan repayments can be funded from profits.						
Applying for any grants available and seeking advice from outside agencies.						
Diversifying early on to avoid overdependence on a few products.						

1 Did you generally agree or disagree, as a group?
2 Were there any ingredients of success that you all agreed or disagreed on?
3 Are there any factors that you think are important which are not on the list?

Raising the finance for growth

Research has shown that business start-ups usually tend to be financed by a combination of personal finance, bank loans and overdrafts, obtained mainly from the high street clearing banks. Business expansion, on the other hand, tends to be financed by the reinvestment of profits, especially in the early stages when the entrepreneur may be wary of borrowing too much and getting into difficulties. However, if a company continues expanding it may get to the point where these reserves or retained profits, ploughed back into the business, are not sufficient to fuel continued growth. An injection of **equity capital** may then be required. Equity is all the firm's capital that is invested in the business – proprietor's own funds in the case of a sole trader or partnership, and shareholders' funds in the case of a limited company. For instance, further equity can provide the funds required to pay for extra factory space and machinery, and for the higher wages and overheads needed to maintain the extra turnover resulting from expansion.

How easy is it to find venture capital, once a decision has been made that an injection of equity is needed? Unfortunately, major investors like the pension funds generally prefer to invest their money in large public companies quoted on the stock exchange, which they perceive as offering a lower risk than small businesses.

In recognition of this situation, the government's **Business Expansion Scheme** has been set up to encourage investment in small firms. Under the scheme, individuals are encouraged to invest between £500 and £40,000 in eligible companies (which are not quoted on the stock exchange). The incentives for them are that they can claim tax relief on their investment and pay no capital gains tax, when the shares are sold, on any profit made. The total acquired must not be more than 30 per cent of the small firm's equity and the investment must be maintained for at least five years.

Venture capitalists, on the other hand, accept that a certain degree of risk is inevitable (as much as a one-in-three failure rate for start-ups), though they tend not to be interested in sums below £50,000 and for some the line is as high as £250,000. They usually hold an equity stake which is between 20 and 40 per cent for their investment, and aim to recoup this when the company goes public, by selling the shareholding. The world's largest source of private investment capital is 3i Group plc. They have helped over 11,000 firms since 1945 and currently have investments in over 3,500 companies.

On a larger scale, the government also has to raise the finance for constantly increasing levels of public expenditure. Industry plays a vital role in creating the wealth to finance these increases.

CASE STUDY

Safety Coatings Ltd – safety in funds

Safety Coatings Ltd was founded in 1978 to exploit a highly innovative technical product. The company applies a tough, clear, plastic coating to glass containers, which protects them during transport and storage and in bottle-washing plants. The contents are also kept intact if the container is accidentally broken. Yet despite having a good product, the company's early growth was hampered by a variety of problems.

One early difficulty was caused by inadequate market research. Along with many other entrepreneurs who have developed a new product, the company assumed that the coated bottles would be readily adopted because of their obvious advantages. But this assumption failed to distinguish a market *need* from a market *requirement*. Most commercial users perceived no immediate need for this innovation, which would double the initial costs of their glassware. Because potential customers' reactions had been wrongly assessed, insufficient attention was given in the marketing plan to the need for educating customers. Though the coating process received excellent exposure when it was featured in *Tomorrow's World* and the *Financial Times*, inadequate funding meant that this was not backed up by a systematic advertising campaign.

The director's reluctance to dilute financial control explains the inadequate start-up capital of £5,000, all of which came from their personal funds. The problem of inadequate funding or **undercapitalisation**, which affected advertising, soon made itself felt elsewhere too. At very short notice, the company's sole supplier of coating powder in the USA stopped manufacture of this essential raw material. Almost overnight, Safety Coatings had to find the necessary funds to buy as large a stock of the powder as possible, which meant having to approach their bank for an overdraft. The company could not afford to ship all the stock from the USA in one go. The cost of storage there and the cost of making part shipments were both affected by changing exchange rates, which played havoc with their cash flow.

The undercapitalisation difficulties were made worse by their limited customer base – five large customers accounted for the majority of turnover. The degree of customer concentration also made the company vulnerable in price negotiations. Many low-volume users were deterred by the company's policy of requiring them to supply their own bottles for coating. Safety Coatings were not able to attract these smaller firms, because they did not have enough capital to build up stock for a service offering ready-coated bottles for these customers.

However, though the early years were fraught with difficulties, the future now looks hopeful. There has been a dramatic improvement in recent trading performance, as one of the three original directors, Valerie Crane, has become sole executive director and been able to implement the changes she would have liked to have made before. Since 1984, turnover has increased by 38 per cent and the workforce has been cut by more than half. The company made a profit in 1985 for the first time.

Source: Peter Chisnall *Small Firms in Action: Case Histories in Entrepreneurship*, McGraw Hill

CASE STUDY

The Body Shop – from little acorns . . .

'I look at what the cosmetics trade is doing and walk in the opposite direction' says Anita Roddick, displaying the kind of unconventional stance that has enabled her to transform The Body Shop from a tiny start-up venture into a multi-national operation within the space of a few short years. From the first shop in Brighton, which was financed by a bank loan of £4,000, Anita Roddick has seen the company she founded in 1976 become something of a retailing legend with a turnover of £195.4 million in 1994. When The Body Shop went public and was floated on the **Unlisted Securities Market (USM)** in 1984, it was valued at £4.75 million. Eight years later the company had out-performed all expectations to achieve a market valuation of £500 million. The exotic-sounding lotions and potions such as Jojoba Moisture Cream, Apricot Lip Balm and Peppermint Foot Lotion are now available in 45 countries worldwide. As their products have gone on sale in over 1,000 shops from New York to Tokyo, the level of overseas profits has led some City analysts to predict that the company's true potential for growth may yet lie ahead.

It was whilst working for the United Nations in the mid-1960s that Anita Roddick first became aware of the effectiveness of natural products. In Sri Lanka she saw how women used pineapple juice as a skin cleanser (later discovering that natural enzymes in the juice help to remove the dead skin cells) and watched the Polynesians using untreated cocoa butter to soften their skins. Back in England she tracked down a herbalist who shared her interest in natural products and together they concocted 20 recipes.

She admits that the reason the products were originally sold in five sizes was because it made the shop look full. Similarly, the use of information cards on the shelves came about because the products were so unusual she realised she ought to explain what each one contained and what it was good for. In fact, the characteristic design features of the shop interiors, which have since come to symbolise The Body Shop style, all resulted from the need to improvise through lack of money. For example, green paint was first used in the Brighton shop because it hid the damp patches!

From the outset, Anita Roddick had a mission – to make The Body Shop the 'most honest cosmetics company in the world'. In an industry that calculatingly chooses the most perfect faces and figures as images for men and women to aspire to, The Body Shop prides itself instead on selling 'well-being'. It aims to 'promote health rather than glamour and reality rather than the dubious promise of instant rejuvenation'. For this reason, the company refuses to make any extravagant claims for its products, other than simply stating their main uses. The atmosphere in the shops mirrors this low-key approach to selling. Sales staff are helpful and knowledgeable, but are trained not to be pushy. Packaging is noticeably plain and functional. Given that the company does not believe in advertising its products, the phenomenal sales record might, at first sight, seem difficult to explain.

In reality, the very absence of advertising hype and of high-pressure sales techniques sets the company apart from its rivals. In the same way, policies such as using products that have not been tested on animals, recycling waste paper, minimising packaging and offering a refill service, all **differentiate** The Body Shop products from those of competitors. In addition, there cannot be many companies who have made as much effort to make consumers aware of important environmental issues, and fewer still who have made as firm a commitment to sourcing raw materials from the developing world.

Clearly, then, there are a number of factors underlying the rapid rate of expansion; the quality and unique nature of the products themselves, the attractiveness of the shops and the strong environmental concern. Less often cited as a contributory factor, but one which has proved significant in the company's growth, is the fact that most of the shops are operated under a **franchise system**. This is where **franchisees** purchase individual shops and the right to sell The Body Shop products, though the company still retains tight control of products, displays, staff training as well as the general operating style of the shops. For example, franchisees are contractually obliged to adopt a local community project, to which each employee is encouraged to devote at least half a day a month during working hours.

The franchise route was chosen initially because the company did not have the capital to expand quickly enough. It was a good decision, as the franchise system provides two benefits: the shops are run as separate enterprises so individual franchisees have an incentive to increase profits; the company does not have a high fixed cost investment in shop buildings and is therefore insulated from the interest rate increases that crippled other retailers during the recent recession. In fact, as far as The Body Shop is concerned, the pace of expansion shows no sign of slackening – every three days a new branch of The Body Shop opens somewhere in the world!

It is perhaps inevitable that this degree of success would attract competition. Yet despite hosts of imitators, The Body Shop continues to lead the field. 'Business is not just about the profit and loss sheet', Anita Roddick is fond of stating. In building a thriving business from scratch in the space of a few short years, she has confounded the sceptics by proving that it is possible for a company to be financially successful as well as socially responsible.

Glossary

Arbitration   where both parties in a dispute agree to accept the decision of an outside body.

Assembly line   where previously manufactured components are brought together and assembled on a production line.

Autocratic leader   one who imposes decisions on subordinates with little or no consultation.

Balance sheet   account which provides a 'snapshot' of the company's financial position at a particular moment in time.

Batch production   where each operation for a batch of goods is completed before the whole batch moves to the next stage.

Break-even point   where costs equal sales revenue and above which companies start to make a profit.

Capital intensive industry   one which requires a high level of investment.

Cash flow   the balance between flows of money coming into and out of a company over a period of time.

Closed shop   where all workers in a company or industry have to belong to one union.

Collateral   the security which is put forward to a lender in order to guarantee payment should the business fail.

Collective bargaining   where unions negotiate with management on behalf of all the employees in a company.

Corporate identity   the image presented by a company.

Contribution   the amount a product contributes to the fixed costs of production, after the variable costs have been taken into account.

Current assets   those assets which are likely to be converted into cash within the next 12 months, such as money from debtors.

Current liabilities   those debts where repayment is due within 12 months, such as overdrafts.

Decentralised management   where authority for decision making is delegated down the organisation to subsidiary companies or divisions.

Democratic leader   one who consults subordinates and involves them in decision making.

Depreciation   the amount by which items like machinery lose value because of their age and through wear and teat.

Diversification   where firms make a variety of products or offer a range of services to avoid 'putting all their eggs in one basket'.

Division of labour   where workers specialise in one operation of the production process.

Economies of scale   where firms are able to cut costs as they increase in size, by being able to operate more efficiently.

Entrepreneur   one who undertakes a risk in a commercial venture.

Equity   all the firms' capital that is invested in the business.

Fixed assets   those assets owned by a company which are not normally sold such as land or buildings.

Fixed costs   costs which do not immediately change with the volume of output.

Flow production   where items move as a continuous flow along the production line.

Footloose industries   light industries which are free to locate anywhere and are not tied to a raw material location.

Fragmentation   where a market becomes split into such small segments that very little profit is generated.

Franchising   where franchisees own the business, but the franchisers provide the name, product and expertise to run it.

Industrial inertia   when an industry continues to locate in an area, even when the original advantages no longer apply.

Issued share capital   the value of shares issued by a company.

Job production   where each item is fully completed before the next one is made.

Just in time   a method of stock control where parts are delivered to the production line only when needed.

Labour intensive industry   one which requires a high input of labour.

Lead time   the time taken to develop a new product until it is ready for full production.

Limited liability   where the responsibility for repaying debts, if the business fails, is restricted to the amount invested.

Line manager   one who is responsible for running a particular department or section.

Liquidity   the ability of a company, through having sufficient current assets, to pay bills as they fall due.

Long term liabilities   those debts where repayment is due after a year, such as bank loans.

Management buy-out   where managers buy out the company they have been working for and then run it as an independent concern.

Market orientation   where firms concentrate on producing the goods the market wants.

Market position   the part of the market which is likely to yield the highest sales for the company.

Market research   where information is gathered on the size and nature of the market.

Market segment   the part of the market which contains a distinct group of buyers, at which the marketing can be targeted.

Mass production   where large volumes of identical products are manufactured at a low unit cost.

Merger   where two firms join together to form a single, larger organisation.

Niche marketing   where firms provide a specialised product or service, rather than catering for the mass market.

Organic growth   where firms expand through their internal growth, rather than by acquiring or merging with other firms.

Overheads   costs which are essential for the general running of the business.

Product life cycle   the stages a product passes through during the time it is available on the market.

Production orientation   where firms concentrate on producing the goods they want to make.

Profit and loss account   account which provides a 'history' of the company's trading fro a given period.

Quality assurance   where firms make sure that the raw materials and parts they use are of good quality, by buying only from reliable suppliers.

Quality control   where firms ensure that their products are of good quality by inspecting out faults.

Reserves   profits which are retained in a business and 'ploughed back' as an investment.

Revenue   income received by a company from its sales and from other sources such as shares in other companies.

Span of control   the number of people for whom a particular manager is responsible.

Tracking study   where a survey is carried out to assess the impact of an advertising campaign by testing consumer recall.

Trade credit   where suppliers allow a period of time for payment.

Undercapitalised   where a firm operates inefficiently because it has not raised enough capital for its requirements.

Unique selling proposition   where a brand is seen as having characteristics which distinguish it from its competitors.

Value added   the amount by which products increase in value in the course of being processed from a raw material to a finished good.

Variable costs   costs which do change with the volume of output.

Venture capital   raised from lenders who accept a higher degree of risk than banks, for instance, but also expects a higher return for their investment.

Work in progress   the valuation of unfinished work in accounts.

Working capital   the capital which is used to fund the firm's day-to-day needs such as for wages, materials etc.

Index

Student Questionnaire on Understanding Industry Sessions

Understanding *Industry*

INSTRUCTIONS: Please mark like this ▬ , using an HB pencil.
Do NOT tick, cross or circle. It is important that you complete the course code.

Student Name:

Date:

School/ College:

COURSE CODE

0	0	0	0	0	0
1	1	1	1	1	1
2	2	2	2	2	2
3	3	3	3	3	3
4	4	4	4	4	4
5	5	5	5	5	5
6	6	6	6	6	6
7	7	7	7	7	7
8	8	8	8	8	8
9	9	9	9	9	9

PART 1 (mark this part after each session)

Did you find the session:

	Interesting						Useful					
	Very 1	2	3	4	5 Not at all		Very 1	2	3	4	5 Not at all	
Introduction	▢	▢	▢	▢	▢		▢	▢	▢	▢	▢	
Marketing	▢	▢	▢	▢	▢		▢	▢	▢	▢	▢	
Finance	▢	▢	▢	▢	▢		▢	▢	▢	▢	▢	
Design & Dev.	▢	▢	▢	▢	▢		▢	▢	▢	▢	▢	
Production	▢	▢	▢	▢	▢		▢	▢	▢	▢	▢	
Personnel	▢	▢	▢	▢	▢		▢	▢	▢	▢	▢	
Management	▢	▢	▢	▢	▢		▢	▢	▢	▢	▢	
Small Business	▢	▢	▢	▢	▢		▢	▢	▢	▢	▢	
Other	▢	▢	▢	▢	▢		▢	▢	▢	▢	▢	
Other	▢	▢	▢	▢	▢		▢	▢	▢	▢	▢	
Summary	▢	▢	▢	▢	▢		▢	▢	▢	▢	▢	

• PRIVATE AND CONFIDENTIAL •

PART 2 (please complete this part at the end of your course)

Do you agree that:

		Agree 1	2	3	4	5 Disagree
1.	The course was interesting	▢	▢	▢	▢	▢
1a.	The course was useful	▢	▢	▢	▢	▢
2.	The UI course has improved my attitude towards industry	▢	▢	▢	▢	▢
3.	The UI course has helped in my studies	▢	▢	▢	▢	▢
4.	The UI course will help in my choice of career	▢	▢	▢	▢	▢
5.	You would recommend the UI course to next year's students	▢	▢	▢	▢	▢
6.	You are likely to discuss the UI course at an interview	▢	▢	▢	▢	▢

		V. Good	Good	Quite Good	Poor	V. Poor
7.	In your opinion, the UI book is:	▢	▢	▢	▢	▢

Why? _____

8. What, in your view, were the best features of the course? _____

_____

Why? _____

9. What were the worst? _____

_____

Why? _____

10. In your opinion, how could the course be improved? _____

_____

11. Your overall comments: _____

_____

_____

DO NOT WRITE HERE

KENDATA Data Entry Technology 01703 869922